The actual lines of a pig (I mean of a really fat pig) are among the loveliest and most luxuriant in nature; the pig has the same great curves, swift and yet heavy, which we see in rushing water or in rolling cloud.
—G. K. Chesterton, *The Uses of Diversity* (1920)

The
Complete
PIG

Sara Rath

Voyageur Press

A TOWN SQUARE BOOK

Edited by Amy Rost-Holtz
Designed by Andrea Rud
Jacket designed by Kristy Tucker
Printed in Hong Kong

00   01   02   03   04   5   4   3   2

Library of Congress Cataloging-in-Publication Data available

ISBN 0-89658-435-6

Distributed in Canada by Raincoast Books
9050 Shaughnessy Street, Vancouver, B.C. V6P 6E5

Published by Voyageur Press, Inc.
123 North Second Street, P.O. Box 338, Stillwater, MN 55082 U.S.A.
651-430-2210, fax 651-430-2211

Educators, fundraisers, premium and gift buyers, publicists, and marketing managers: Looking for creative products and new sales ideas? Voyageur Press books are available at special discounts when purchased in quantities, and special editions can be created to your specifications. For details contact the marketing department at 800-888-9653.

Page 1: A Berkshire sow, primed for the fair (1950s). (Minnesota State Fair collection)

Page 2: Playful piglet. (Photograph © Jim Steinbacher, courtesy of Leslie Levy Creative Art Licensing, Scottsdale, AZ)

Page 3: Snouty smooch and giggles. (Photograph © J. C. Allen & Son Inc., West Lafayette, IN)

Page 6: Sunspotted pigs. (Photograph © Alan and Sandy Carey)

Dedication

For Jocelyn & Christopher

Acknowledgments

Librarians are invaluable resources for writers, and I owe my gratitude to James Gollata at the University of Wisconsin–Richland and Willa Schmidt at the University of Wisconsin–Madison; when all else failed, they offered their friendship, support, and reference information. Thanks also to my neighborhood Elm Grove Library for their ready and welcome assistance. Judy Rose, host of "Simply Folk" at Wisconsin Public Radio helped research pig folksongs. Allison Tremblay provided the "How to Say Pig in Different Languages" list. Andrew Wilson, a.k.a. "The Oracle," answered mythological queries over the Internet, and the amazing "Porkopolis" website provided enough swine minutiae to choke a hog. As always, my husband, Del Lamont, and children, Jay Rath and Laura Beausire, cheered me on when I began to wallow.

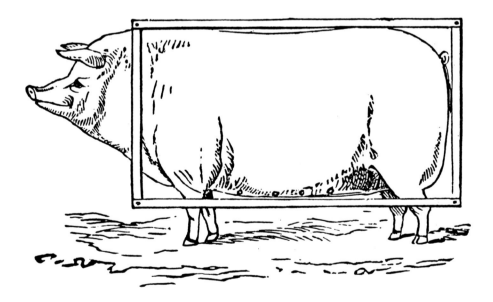

"Testing the Form of a Pig," from *Harris on the Pig*, by Joseph Harris (1889).

Contents

To Market, To Market

To market, to market, to buy a fat pig.
Home again, home again, jiggety-jig.
—Anonymous nursery rhyme

Bluebacks
Facing page: Also known as bluebutts, blue-backs is a colloquial name for an unusual crossbreed. These pigs are a Hampshire/ Yorkshire/Duroc cross, with distinctive blue-black freckles on pink skin, and are found at the Great Bend Organic Farm, Port Clinton, Pennsylvania. (Photograph © David Lorenz Winston)

To market, to market . . .
Inset: Postcard, circa 1907.

"This little pig went to market. This little pig stayed home. . . ."

I was playing "This Little Pig" with my new grandson when I had a realization: The first little pig, the one who went "to market," was not on his way to the grocery store! For well over two centuries, this rhyme, the best-known toe- or finger-counting rhyme in the English language, has perpetuated that myth to generations of unsuspecting toddlers who giggled while Mommy tickled and tweaked each tiny toe or finger in turn. "This Little Pig" may well have been our first exposure to poetry—or to pigs.

I also reached the conclusion, after much scrutiny and meditation, that this seemingly innocuous Mother Goose rhyme may have been our first lesson in the dreaded Seven Deadly Sins: Pride, Covetousness, Lust, Envy, Gluttony, Anger, and Sloth.

Whereupon the Five Little Pigs Meet the Seven Deadly Sins

This little pig went to market,
This little pig stayed home....

It sounds innocent, doesn't it? Well, so does "Hey diddle diddle / The cat and the fiddle," which is really about Queen Elizabeth I. Little Miss Muffet, who "Sat on a tuffet . . . ," was an unflattering comment about Mary Queen of Scots. Many rhymes, fables, and fairy tales that seem quaint to us were composed as allegories to provoke political dissent or provide discourse in moral rectitude.

It's not wildly improbable to believe these "little piggy" lines harken back to the sixth century when St. Gregory the Great came up with his catalog of seven moral offenses. The Seven Deadly Sins became a popular theme in medieval morality plays and works of art, providing grist for Dante, Chaucer, Shakespeare, and other literary giants, including Mother Goose.

During the eleventh through thirteenth centuries, the sow and the boar symbolized a number of despicable vices in *Bestiaries*, collections of moralized fables about animals—both real and imagined—that were intended as suitable text for sermons or uplifting words of advice. Around 1500, Hieronymus Bosch depicted a sow in a nun's habit embracing a man in his famous painting, *The Garden of Worldly Delights*. This image has been recognized as a depiction of avarice or greed. In the same painting there are a number of other pigs who represent sins of the flesh.

Many historic English churches are decorated with diminutive carvings of pigs, copied by ancient wood carvers from illustrated manuscripts or Books of Hours. In these carvings, sows often play musical instruments, such as the harp or bagpipes, and serenade their piglets. (In some countries, a sow's teats are referred to as her "set of bagpipes.") Carvings of the sow suckling her piglets were intended to remind parishioners of tithing—that a tenth of each man's worldly wealth, as represented by pigs, belonged to the church.

Let's have a look at an earlier version of "This Little Pig," published in the most influential collection of nursery rhymes ever written, *Mother Goose's Melody; or Sonnets for the Cradle*. This rhyme dates back to 1781 (or before) and addresses all ten fingers or toes:

Let us go the wood, says this little
  pig;
What to do there? Says that pig;
To look for my mother, says this pig;
What to do with her? Says that pig;
Kiss her to death, says this pig.
This pig went to the barn.
This ate all the corn.
This said he wouldn't tell.
This said he wasn't well.
This went week, week, week, over the
  door sill.

The editor of *Mother Goose's Melody* appended this maxim to the rhyme: "If

---

"Never eat more than you can lift."
—Miss Piggy

Pig sign at Nantucket, Massachusetts restaurant. (Photograph © Leslie M. Newman)

ENTRANCE

THIS LITTLE PIG

A Tale in Five Curls.

This little pig
From *A Tale in Five Curls*, published in 1880: "This little Pig went to market, the weather was warm and clear, / And he gamboled along, with a laugh and a song, / At the side of his mother dear. . . ."

we do not govern our passions our passions will govern us."

And so we arrive at the more familiar, albeit still centuries-old version: *This little pig went to market.*

He did so with **Pride**, of course. The big toe or thumb, a real porker compared to the rest of the digits and certainly more powerful, marched off to market while his lesser litter mates had to fall back upon their innate personalities to cope with his good fortune.

Morality plays of the fourteenth century commonly told the story of a pilgrimage in which the subject encountered a range of temptations. In this case, as always, "pride goeth before a fall." Pride comes first among the Deadly

Wall Street, known today for the trading of stocks and bonds, was originally home to herds of free-roaming hogs bred by colonial New York farmers. In their desire to limit the forays of the hogs, residents of Manhattan erected a long, permanent wall along the northern edge of what is now Lower Manhattan (then known as New Amsterdam) in 1653. A street eventually ran along the inside of this wall and was named, of course, "Wall Street."

Three little pigs
"Once upon a time there were three little pigs. . . ." (Photograph © Jim Steinbacher, courtesy of Leslie Levy Creative Art Licensing, Scottsdale, AZ)

Seven, Catholic scholars claim, because it is the source of all the other deadly or "cardinal" sins. "This little pig [who] went to market" is preordained to meet the butcher's knife.

This little pig stayed home.

The second little pig, the one who was left behind, ignorantly **Coveted** his brother's trip into town. He has yet to learn how dangerous the market can be for a plumpish pig. In the 1880 children's book, *This Little Pig: A Tale in Five Curls*, the second little pig is "a lazy little Pig" because "he twiddles his thumbs, and won't do his sums, And he can't say his A B C." In addition to covetousness, Mama Pig accuses her second little pig of **Sloth**. His bedroom was probably a pigsty.

This little pig had roast beef,
This little pig had none.

Aha, the curse of **Gluttony!** Dante, who addressed these seven mortal vices in his *Divine Comedy* celebrated the sin of gluttony in his *Inferno*'s Third Circle of Hell, where one of the gluttons wallowing in garbage is named Ciacco, "the Hog."

It's only fair to toss in some **Envy** for the little pig who had none. In a Victorian trading card from the turn of the century, a pig with a rib roast under his arm perches on top of the appropriate digit; he is brandishing a silver knife and

wearing a white napkin tied around his neck. The envious little pig on the adjacent fingertip wears a hopeful expression, but we know he won't sample a morsel of that succulent slab.

This little pig cried wee wee wee
All the way home.

Who would not feel sympathy for the fifth little pig? The itsy-bitsy pinky is only expressing his **Anger** at being the runt of the litter with a temper tantrum of porcine proportions. This little pig who cried "wee wee wee" warns that life's pilgrimage is fraught with dismay. In Norwich Cathedral (Norfolk, England), in a wood carving dated approximately 1480, Anger is portrayed as a soldier, riding on the back of a boar. (In the same cathedral, "Greed" rides on the back of a sow.)

There you have it: Five Little Pigs and six of the Deadly Sins; only **Lust** remains to be discovered.

Sometimes defined as "hankering for impure pleasures" by the church (see the 1781 rhyme, ". . . *to look for my mother . . . kiss her to death*"), Lust may also be looked at as "a passionate or overmastering desire" or "ardent enthusiasm." But the clue to the presence of Lust in *This Little Piggie* is so simple as to be overlooked: In Europe the symbol for licentiousness, or Lust, is THE PIG.

Hogwash:
A Rebuttal of Sins Attributed to Said Little Pigs, Above

I don't want to pick a fight with Mother Goose, but the old bird would be hard pressed to justify her association of the Seven Deadly Sins with the swine we know and love today.

Pig Futures

There's a lot more to a pig than pork chops and bacon. Hog by-products have played a vital though less-visible role in maintaining and improving the quality of human life for generations (that's *human* generations), and the scientific and technological development of new medical and industrial applications are constantly being developed.

Industrial and consumer products developed from pigs may not be glamorous, but they cannot be synthetically duplicated. Pigskin is probably the best known and is utilized in high quality leather goods, sporting goods, and upholstery.

The remaining list goes on practically *ad infinitum*. From pig blood we get plywood adhesive, protein source in feeds, and fabric printing and dyeing ingredients. From bones and skin there are glue, buttons, and bone china. Bone meal provides fertilizer, glass, water filters, porcelain enamel, and a mineral source in feed. Pig bristles are used for artists' brushes, insulation, and upholstery. Meat scraps are used in commercial feeds and pet food. Fatty acids and glycerine become insecticides, floor waxes, weed killers, water-proofing agents, lubricants, cement, oil polishes, rubber, crayons, cosmetics, chalk, antifreeze, matches, putty, and linoleum. And then there are pig gallstones, which are sometimes used as ornaments!

But pharmaceuticals rank second only to meat in the important contributions pigs make to society. Insulin, for example, taken from the pig's pancreas, is used in the treatment of diabetes. Hog insulin is especially advantageous since the chemical structure most nearly resembles that found in the human component.

Since 1971, tens of thousands of pig heart valves have been used to replace damaged or diseased heart valves in human recipients of all ages.

Skin from hogs, because of its similarity to human skin, is specially selected and treated so "porcine burn dressings" may be used to treat victims of massive burns.

Those are perhaps the most widely known medical uses for pig by-products, but you may have utilized others yourself, for hogs are the source of nearly forty common drugs and pharmaceuticals including cortisone, epinephrine, fetal pig plasma, heparin, estrogen, progesterone, pepsin, thyroxin, melatonin, and thyroid-stimulating hormone.

Xenotransplantation is the newest wrinkle in biotechnology to help ease the shortage of transplant organs for human use. *Xeno* means foreign, so Xenotransplantation refers to the transplant of animal parts to humans. According to the Department of Health and Human Services, at least 4,000 Americans die each year while waiting for transplants, but pigs are coming to the rescue.

Pig organs are the right size for adult humans, and the use of pig heart valves (which are treated and therefore do not contain living cells) has proven tremendously successful. Rejection in human-to-human transplants is managed with immunosuppressive drugs. Pig-to-human transplants run into difficulty, however, when human antibodies identify pig sugar antigens on the transplanted organ and set off an inflammatory reaction that can destroy the organ in less than an hour.

Clinical trials are proceeding cautiously, until the risk of cross-species infection is determined and cloning of pigs is easily accomplished. Researchers hope that within fifteen years, humans will be able to receive permanent organ transplants from swine. But even if Xenotransplantation becomes readily available, scientists anticipate an inevitable ethical challenge: Should humans share their innards with animals, and does raising pigs for their organs constitute cruelty to animals?

A pig trotting off to market does not leave its farmer living high off the hog right now. "Raising hogs these days is like going to town and throwing $10 bills out the window," a Corn Belt farmer complained in a 1999 *Milwaukee Journal Sentinal* article. In 1998 hog prices plummeted to record lows not seen since the Civil War, and the nation is suffering from a glut of pork. "Too Many Piggies Went to Market," read a headline in the January 7, 1999, *New York Times*. Gone are the days when pigs were popularly known as "mortgage lifters," when farmers' debts were relieved because of the way pigs can multiply: In only three months, three weeks, and three days one pig can produce a litter of eight or more, and in six months a competent farmer will have them ready to sell.

Smiles of contentment
A young girl and a young pig enjoy each other's company. (Photograph © J. C. Allen & Son Inc., West Lafayette, IN)

As for the second little pig, the slothful one, hogs have always been given a bum rap when it comes to their reputation for slovenliness. If given a choice, a pig will not roll around in its own filth. And you can never really "sweat like a pig," because pigs do not perspire. Their need to regulate their body temperature by wallowing in muddy waters during hot weather has muddied the pig's name.

Gluttony? That concept is consistent with the ubiquitous image of the pig who roots around garbage and hogs his fill of swill. In olden days, pigs did wander through the village in search of table scraps, mill wastes, and spilled grains, but today's hogs bulk up by daily consuming three percent of their body weight in special diets designed to get them off to market in record time. If you ever really "eat like a pig," you'd be sorry: Pigs put on one pound of weight for every three pounds of feed they consume!

Covetousness? Envy? Name another animal that so generously and conveniently—to say nothing of genetically—is able to share its internal organs with us. Since 1971, tens of thousands of hog heart valves have been surgically implanted in humans to replace those weakened by disease or injury. Pig organs happen to be just the right size for adult humans. Pig-to-man (or woman) transplants have proven so successful that scientists are now injecting human DNA into fertilized pig eggs to create "transgenic" pigs that will allow transplants of entire hog hearts and other organs with less possibility for rejection.

It is true that pigs can get angry. The ferocity of wild boars is legendary. Early in the fifteenth century, Edward, second Duke of York, wrote ". . . the wild boar slayeth a man at one stroke as with a knife, and therefore he can slay any other beast sooner than they could slay him. It is a proud beast and fierce and perilous. . . ."

And there's no getting around the fact that pigs are fecund, although their propensity for lust may be exaggerated. *The Biggle Swine Book* (1906) advises, "A boar fully grown and properly fed may be allowed to serve two sows a day for several days in succession, if necessary, but this should not be continued indefinitely if the best results are to be expected. About one sow a day on an average is about the limit."

Where There's Swill, There's a Way

Xenophanes, a Greek philosopher (570–475 B.C.), wrote, "If horses could paint they would draw gods like horses." I'd like to suggest that if pigs could paint, they would be justified in drawing gods that resembled pigs.

Although maligned through the ages, in truth, the pig has a proud heritage. Pigs are the most ancient of nonruminant mammals and were on this earth forty million years ago. On a recent episode of PBS-TV's *Nature*, scientists affirmed that "every continent bears the imprint of pig's feet . . . pigs are unique as one of the only large mammals that exists, in one form or another, in every part of the world."

Today's popular culture introduces us to pigs that are entertaining and sweet, heroes and tyrants. Pigs are smart. Pigs can be housebroken. Cows may remind us of mothers, horses may convey a regal sense of dignity, and sheep surely are soft and cuddly to hug. But that little pig who trots off to market has won the respect of the ages.

Other than humans, pigs are the only creatures that will consistently and willingly imbibe alcohol for purposes of scientific study.

Cleaning the sty
Pigs have an undeserved reputation for slovenliness. (BIZARRO © 1989 by Dan Piraro. Reprinted with permission of Universal Press Syndicate. All rights reserved.)

BIZARRO/By Piraro

GEE. I GUESS I HAD YOU GUYS ALL WRONG.

PIRARO. © CHRONICLE FEATURES 1989   7-28

Swineherd covered with litter
This good farmer truly loves his pigs. (Photograph © J. C. Allen & Son Inc., West Lafayette, IN)

"Lawsuit, n. A machine which you go into as a pig and come out as a sausage."
—Ambrose Bierce, *The Devil's Dictionary* (1906)

Bringing Home the Bacon

There is some dispute over the origin of the word *bacon*. Some suggest it is a corruption of the Scottish word *baken*, which means "dried." Others feel it is derived from *beechen*, as the finest bacon was thought to be obtained from pigs fattened by the fruit of the beech tree. In the old Lancashire dialect, the word "bacon" is spelled and pronounced "beechen."

In England, a side of bacon was referred to as a *flitch*. In the year 1111, a British woman named Juga, purportedly an aristocrat, is thought to have been the originator of the custom of "flitching," or kneeling on sharp stones at the doorway of a church while swearing to have been happily married for the past twelve months. In so doing, and by promising no arguments or desire for separation, the practice of presenting said woman with a side or "flitch" of bacon was developed and continued, off and on, from medieval times until 1855.

Danish bacon

Denmark has more pigs than people, and bacon is one of its most valuable agricultural exports. According to author Valerie Porter (*Pigs: A Handbook to Breeds of the World,* 1993), "The Danish pig was tailormade to produce bacon for the British plate, in a national breeding scheme that began in earnest at the turn of the century. . . . Farmers were encouraged to use the best bred stock, the boars of which were subsidised by the bacon co-operatives." By 1980, Denmark had a population of ten million pigs. Today Denmark has 125 private pig breeding farms where four purebred lines are raised: Danish Landrace, Danish Large White, Danish Duroc, and Danish Hampshire.

What! you don't know how to spell Bacon.
why - D.A.N.I.S.H!

"*Edible, adj.* Good to eat, and wholesome to digest, as a worm to a toad, a toad to a snake, a snake to a pig, a pig to a man, and a man to a worm."
—Ambrose Bierce, *The Devil's Dictionary* (1906)

Racing pigs
Above: "Robinson's Racing Pigs" leap obstacles during a mad dash at the Michigan Spree Festival, Livonia, Michigan. (Photograph © Keith Baum/BaumsAway!)

Porket, porculus
Facing page: "Porket. Porculus, a pygg, a shoote, i.e. shot, a young pig."
—*Thesaurus Linguae Romanae et Britannicae*, Thomas Cooper (1565) (Photograph © Jim Steinbacher, courtesy of Leslie Levy Creative Art Licensing, Scottsdale, AZ)

"There is a tragic color to the pig. Pigs are reviled, but somehow, having been bred for meat, they haven't lost their intelligence across all these generations. I'm just blown away by that. So I can't look at a pig now without a sense of reverence. Because they are metaphorical for all of us who are ultimately mortal."
—George Miller, director of the films
Babe and *Babe: Pig in the City*

Chapter 1

The Pig: A Paradox

There warn't anybody at the church, except maybe a hog or two, for there warn't any lock on the door, and hogs like a puncheon floor in summertime because it's cool. If you notice, most folks don't go to church only when they've got to; but a hog is different.
—Mark Twain,
Adventures of Huckleberry Finn (1884)

Some pig
Facing page: "When Charlotte's web said SOME PIG, Wilbur tried hard to look like some pig."
—*Charlotte's Web*, E. B. White (1952) (Photograph © Lynn M. Stone)

Glædelig Jul!
Inset: Pigs traditionally represent good luck and prosperity in some European countries. In the early twentieth century, pigs were frequently depicted on postcards as symbols of good fortune and warm wishes.

In a very old fable, a wolf is about to devour a pig when the pig reminds the wolf that it's Friday, and good Catholics don't eat meat on Friday. They converse a bit more and the wolf eventually says to the pig, "They seem to call you by many names."

"Yes," the pig replies, "I am called swine, grunter, hog, and I know not what besides. The Latins call me porcus."

"Porpus, do they?" says the wolf with a wily grin, "Well, a porpoise is a fish, and we may eat fish on a Friday." Then the wolf devours the pig without another word.

According to scholars, the phrase "The Latins call me porcus" has come to be used as a sly rebuke to anyone who is boasting, showing off, or trying to make himself appear more important than he actually is.

Porcus, swine, hog, pig: All refer to a rotund oval-shaped mammal that has a pretty distinguished history. Tiptoeing on slender legs, this member of the family *Suidae* has planted its wee cloven hoof prints in mud all over this planet for at least forty million years (compared to the paltry million years that humans have populated the globe). Unfortunately, in addition to its notable ancestry, the pig has also inherited a perplexing reputation.

Some authorities say the word "hog" comes from the Old English *hogg*, the original meaning of which has been lost through the ages. One source claims "hog" is derived from a Celtic word meaning "swine," which is based on an Indo-European root meaning "pig."

Well, what about "pig"? There's the Old English *picga*. From the fourteenth to sixteenth century a pig was known as *Pygge*. In Middle English (from the thirteenth to seventeenth century), the term was spelled *pigge*, but in the sixteenth century it became *pyg*. *Porc* is pig in Old French; *bigge* is pig in Low German and Early Modern Dutch. For a different point of view, consider *Verres*, Latin for *boar*.

A twelfth-century bestiary has this to say: "The sow is so named (sus) because it roots up (subigat) the pastures, that is, it seeks its food by rooting up the ground. Boars are so named (verres) because they have great strength (vires). The pig (porcus), as if named from 'spurcus' (filthy), wallows, for it buries itself in filth and mud and covers itself with mire."

Sportsmen in the Middle Ages spoke of a herd of harts and other deer; a bevy of roes; a sloth of bear; a sounder of wild swine; a singular of boars; a drift of tame swine.

In his 1576 publication, *Noble Arte of Venerie or Hunting*, George Turberville wrote:

A young boar that has come into the third year of age is said to have "lately left the Sounder." He never leaves the Sounder until three years at least. The next year he is a Bore. The next year after that he is a . . . Syngular. A Bore that left the Sounder four or five years since is a Swine Royall. If asked where he fed the night before, one may answer—in the fieldes or in the meades or in the corne. If you see definitely that he has been in any meddow or corne close, then say he has been "rowting or worming" in such a fielde or meddow. When he feeds in a tuft of Fern, then you shall say 'he hathe rowted the Fearne' or hathe 'broken into the Parke.' Anything he eats except fearne or rootes is called feeding—they are called "rowting or worming." He has been "mowsing" when he breaks into a Barn or Granary, for corn, acorns, pease & such which mice eat. When he "rowteth" not, then shall you say he "graseth."

Drawing his own conclusion
Postcard advertising Marsh & Baxter sausage.

Yorkshire grazing
A healthy adult Yorkshire grazes at Hewitt Farm, Spring City, Pennsylvania. (Photograph © David Lorenz Winston)

"In his (or her) lifetime the average Briton eats 7 cattle, 36 sheep, 36 pigs, and 550 poultry. Imagine seeing this sizeable herd in a field—and being told that you would have to eat your way through them!"
—David Jacobs, in *RSPCA Today* (Spring 1983)

The Year of the Pig

Year of the Pig
Sincerity, tolerance and honesty,
12th year of the Chinese calendar.

Were You Born Under the Sign of the Pig?

30 January 1911 to 17 January 1912
16 February 1923 to 4 February 1924
4 February 1930 to 23 January 1936
22 January 1947 to 9 February 1948
8 February 1959 to 27 January 1960
27 January 1971 to 14 February 1972
13 February 1983 to 1 February 1984
31 January 1995 to 18 February 1996
(Lunar Year: 4693)
(future years: 2007 and 2019)

"Year of the pig" artwork

Design for artwork on the "First Day Cover" done by noted Chinese artist Zhan Gengxi.

The Personality of the Pig

The Pig is born under the sign of honesty. He has a kind and understanding nature and is well known for his abilities as a peacemaker. He hates any sort of discord or unpleasantness and will do all in his power to work out differences of opinion or bring opposing factions together. He is an excellent conversationalist and speaks truthfully and to the point. He dislikes any form of falsehood or hypocrisy and is a firm believer in justice and the maintenance of law and order.

Famous Pigs: Woody Allen, Julie Andrews, Fred Astaire, Humphrey Bogart, Maria Callas, Noel Coward, Oliver Cromwell, Ralph Waldo Emerson, William Randolph Hearst, Ernest Hemingway, Henry VIII, Alfred Hitchcock, Elton John, C. G. Jung, Stephen King, Henry Kissinger, John McEnroe, Johnny Mathis, Dan Quayle, Ronald Reagan, Albert Schweitzer, Steven Spielberg, Tracey Ullman, Sarah the Duchess of York.

"Year of the Pig" stamp

Issued December 30, 1994, in honor of the Year of the Pig, celebrated in 1995. The Chinese lunar calendar is represented by a different animal each year in twelve-year cycles. The pig is the twelfth. According to legend, the Heavenly Jade Emperor summoned all the world's animals to a race, and the pig came in last (the rat came in first).

The Maligned Swine

Geographically, it is felt that swine originated in Asia. In *Pigs: A Handbook to Breeds of the World* (1993), Valerie Porter explains that the domesticated pig eventually "radiated from its south west Asian cradle. It spread southwards, into ancient Syria, into the Jordan valley's Jericho and into Palestine. Pork was still on the menu for Jewish religious rites during the Bronze Age. By the end of the fifth millennium there were domesticated pigs in Egypt, and there were large herds being bred in the Nile Valley around 1500 B.C. From ancient Egypt the domesticated pig went into Sudan, where it was still common in 1173 A.D." Accompanying nomadic pastoralists, the pig also spread into Greece and southeast Europe.

Although it is clear domestic pigs appeared in many cultures throughout ancient history, their Asian origin is disputed by some experts. A definitive text, Charles W. Towne and Edward N. Wentworth's *Pigs: From Cave to Corn Belt* (1950), states, "[F]rom the Tertiary through the mid-Pleistocene, the outwardly radiating waves of fossils, spreading from centers around the Alps, make Europe appear to be the cradle from which wild swine evolved."

Their bristles afford little protection from cold, and without sweat glands or other cooling apparatus, pigs are subject to problems with heat. Swine fossils are absent in the deserts and plains, but many traces have been discovered in the cool, swampy forests that provided a congenial habitat for their survival.

So we are not exactly certain who first tamed the pig. We are confident that the domestic hog descended from the wild boar, but it is unknown whether its ancestors are one particular kind of wild boar or several species. However, it is clear why the pig was first domesticated. Unlike other farm animals (the cow, sheep, horse, and chicken, for example) the pig is useless during its lifetime. Whoever tamed the pig must have had a pork roast in mind.

The Pig in China

The pig became domesticated in China around 5000 B.C. In Imperial China, the pig was a good luck symbol, and around 4000 B.C., when fresh pork enjoyed royal status, the emperor decreed that the Chinese people were to raise and breed hogs. The earliest surviving recipe for suckling pig dates back to China and was written around 500 B.C. Chinese tombs as early as the Chou period (1122–221 B.C.) contained miniature pig models carved from jade or other precious stones, which had been placed in the hands of the dead to guarantee the prosperity of the deceased. Entire herds of swine were sometimes buried in Chinese tombs to ensure a fresh supply of pork in the afterlife.

Today, China is the number one producer and consumer of fresh pork in the world. The pig is honored by the Chinese, who assign the Year of the Pig to the twelfth year of their lunar calendar. This came about when the Heavenly Jade Emperor held a race in which all the world's animals were invited to participate. The first twelve to complete the race were assigned years in order of their finish. The pig was in twelfth place. Those born during the Year of the Pig, sometimes referred to as the Year of the Boar, are reputed to be sedate and easy going, sincere,

Just the good old wish, In the good old way
"A Happy and Prosperous New Year"
1918
JOHN MORRELL & CO.
OTTUMWA, IA.

tolerant, and honest. Unfortunately, they are also somewhat naive as they expect others to be endowed with those traits, too. In the future, the years 2007 and 2019 will each be a Year of the Pig in the Chinese lunar calendar.

The Pig in Ancient Greece and Rome

In ancient Italy, herds of swine dined on acorns in the valley of the river Po. Immense herds of swine intermingled in the forests of Tuscany and Lombardy during the second century B.C., and the swineherds had a unique way of calling their own: each swineherd carried a horn, a blast from which his own hogs recognized and "came trooping to him with such vehemence that nothing could stop them."

Greek mythology reveals Adonis was killed by a wild boar while hunting. Attis and Osiris were also slain by boars. Wor-

"Happy New Year!"
Promotional calendar card from Morell & Co. Because they were considered symbols of prosperity and good luck at the close of the nineteenth century, pigs provided lucky charms by illustrating calendars and business cards.

"It is better to be Socrates dissatisfied than a pig satisfied."
—John Stuart Mill, 1806–1873,
Utilitarianism (1863)

Forbidden Flesh

Forbidden to you for food are: dead meat, blood and the flesh of the swine and that which hath been invoked the name other than Allah.
—Holy Koran 5:4

The religion of Islam is similar to Judaism with regard to dietary laws and pork. The Koran forbids "only that which dieth of itself, and blood, and swine's flesh."

In Hindu mythology, the god Vishnu turns into the cosmic boar, Varahavatara, in one of his many incarnations. Kali, the Hindu Mother-Goddess, is represented as a black sow who gives birth to the world and then eats her offspring, perpetuating the endless cycle of life. And an Indian creation legend depicts the god Brahma, in the form of a boar, lifting up the earth on his back from the waters of the primeval flood. Adherents of Hinduism eat no pork or pig meat products of any kind, and Sikhs eat very little pork. Ironically, because pork is generally regarded as taboo in India, feral pigs freely roam village streets where they act as informal street cleaners and, as such, are given special protection.

Pigs, dreaming

In his radio play *Under Milk Wood* (1954), Welsh poet Dylan Thomas declared that on lazy afternoons, pigs "smile as they snort and dream. They dream of the acorned swill of the world, the rooting for pig-fruit, the bagpipe dugs of the mother sow, the squeal and snuffle of yesses of the women pigs in rut. They mud-bask and snout in the pig-loving sun; their tails curl; they rollick and slobber and snore to deep, smug, after-swill sleep." (Photograph © Keith Baum/BaumsAway!)

Even a baby pig a few hours old is capable of putting up a piercing squealing, audible half-a-mile away. This little animal is the noisiest of all babies, and is almost always squealing unless it is either glued to a teat or delightfully asleep.

shipers of both Attis and Adonis abstained from eating pork. Myths that portray a hero or god being gored in the groin by a boar purportedly refer to ritual castration.

According to legend in Crete, even mighty Zeus was slain by a boar. Among the animals said to have suckled him was the sow.

At the time of corn planting, Greeks sacrificed pigs to Demeter, the goddess of agriculture (mythologists hypothesize that the pig may have been Demeter herself in animal form). Pigs were sacred to Demeter, sometimes known as "Phorcis the Sow," and she is often portrayed as carrying or accompanying a pig. The choice of the pig for sacrifice may have been out of either respect or punishment,

for pigs were responsible for rooting up and ravaging her crops. An alternate opinion claims the pigs should have been praised, because their rooting tilled the ground and thus prepared the soil for planting. The Demeter pig-sacrifice ceremony was often chosen to illustrate Greek vases.

Pigs also had a role in Hades' rape of Demeter's daughter, Persephone. The swineherd, Eubuleus, was tending his herd in the area when the earth opened up, swallowing Persephone and his pigs. Eubuleus reported this catastrophe to Demeter, who rewarded him with a gift of corn. Each year the story was re-enacted at the festival of the Thesmorphoria at Eleusis, where pigs were tossed into a cavern and the remains of pigs

Greek boar hunt
According to Greek mythology, Adonis was killed by a wild boar while hunting. Therefore, the ritual boar sacrifice was made to Aphrodite, Adonis's lover. The priests of Adonis may have covered themselves with boar skins during these sacrificial slayings.

thrown there the year before were used to fertilize the crops.

The Roman poet Ovid (43 B.C.–A.D. 17) wrote how Meleager slew the Calydonian boar in what is perhaps the most famous account of the Calydonian boar hunt. The Fates appeared before Althaea, the mother of Meleager, shortly after his birth. They told her that her son would die when a log, which was burning on the hearth at that moment, had burned out. Hearing this, Althaea extinguished the log and hid it in a chest. Years later, when Meleager returned from his search for the Golden Fleece, the young man vowed to kill the monstrous boar that was devastating Calydon. To hunt the boar, Meleager gathered many of the noblest Greek heroes, including Atalanta, daughter of the Boeotian king Schoeneus. After several heroes had been killed, Atalanta was the first to wound the boar. Meleager gave the boar the coup de grâce, and therefore received the boar's skin, which he presented to Atalanta, whom he loved. Such an act was an insult to his uncles, the brothers of Althaea, who were slighted at being given less honor than a girl, so a quarrel ensued and Meleager killed his uncles. When this news reached his mother Althaea, she took the unburned log from its chest and cast it on the fire. As the log was consumed, Meleager's life waned and he died.

A portion of the Greek myths of creation involved a ritual of cleansing. This ritual included the slaying of a suckling pig so that its blood might be poured over the hands of the guilty murderer, who sat in silence at the hearth while Zeus was invoked as the Purifier.

The oldest mystery cult of ancient Greece was known as the Eleusinian Mysteries, and bathing in the sea, an important element of the cult's ritual initiation, was a purificatory rite. On the second day of the cult's Greater Mysteries, each initiate would rush toward the sea with a small pig in his arms. In an act of ritual cleansing, they had to wash themselves and the pig. Following the ritual bath, the pigs would be sacrificed and the pig-blood was considered a potent cleansing agent against demonic evil.

The Greek poet Homer (eighth century B.C.) was the first to make a written

In the forty million years of its existence, most of the pig's evolutionary modification has taken place in its digestive system, due to the change in diet that has helped to keep it alive.

A good bath

"There is nothing a pig loves more than a good bath," says British author Barbara Woodhouse in *Talking to Animals* (1954). "There is something delightfully lovable about a really clean pig, in clean yellow straw." (Minnesota State Fair collection)

reference to wild and domesticated pigs. In this passage from *The Odyssey* (translated by W. H. D. Rouse), he told the famous and tragic story of the sorceress Circe, who lured Ulysses's men to her island of Aiaia and changed them into swine:

> There Circê lived, a terrible goddess with lovely hair, who spoke in the language of men, own sister to murderous Aietas; their father was Helios, who gives light to mankind, and their mother was Persê, a daughter of Oceanos. . . .
>
> They stopt at the outer doors of the courtyard, and heard the beautiful goddess within singing in a lovely voice, as she worked at the web on her loom, a large web of incorruptible stuff, a glorious thing of delicate gossamer fabric, such as goddesses make. The silence was broken by Politês, who was nearest and dearest to me of all my companions, and the most trusty. He said:
>
> "Friends I hear a voice in the house, some woman singing prettily at the loom, and the whole place echoes with it. Goddess or woman, let's go in and speak to her."
>
> Then they called her loudly. She came out at once, and opened the shining doors, and asked them to come in; they all followed her, in their innocence, only Eurylochos remained behind, for he suspected a trap. She gave them all comfortable seats, and made them a posset, cheese and meal and pale honey mixt with Pramneian wine; but she put dangerous drugs in the mess, to make them wholly forget their native land. When they had swallowed it, she gave them a tap of her wand at once and herded them into pens; for now they had pigs' heads and grunts and bristles, pigs all over except that their minds were the same as before. There they were then, miserably shut up in the pigsty. Circê threw them a lot of beechnuts and acorns and cornel-beans to eat, such as the earth-bedded swine are used to.

The Pig in Ancient Egypt

In Ancient Egypt, the pig represented both the spirit of Osiris when fields were sown and the spirit of Seth when they were harvested. As beloved as the pig may have been in the fields, it was considered unclean. If a person touched a pig, he or she was expected to wash off the taint immediately by entering the waters of the nearest river, clothes and all. Furthermore, it was believed that one could contract leprosy by drinking pig's milk.

The poor swineherd was regarded with more contempt than the pig itself. "Swineherd" became a synonym for someone who was rude and ignorant and had "swinish" characteristics. The swineherd was denied entrance to temples and was not allowed to marry outside his ranks.

Although the pig was maligned, reviled, and denounced as a foul and odious animal, Egyptian pig images date back to 3400 B.C. The Greek historian Herodotus (484–425 B.C.) and biographer Plutarch (A.D. 46–120) argue that the Egyptian's antipathy toward swine was actually sanctity, for, paradoxically, the pig was considered sacred in Egypt. Ancient Egyptian papyri invested pig's

Tantric Buddhists worship Marici, the Diamond Sow.

Pig iron, produced during the fifteenth century, is so-named because the molten metal is cast into a series of stubby, round ingots known as "pigs," which resemble a row of suckling piglets at their mother's teats.

Quality time with Mom
The herd size of a hog farm is usually measured by the number of breeding sows. (Photograph © Alan and Sandy Carey)

blood with medicinal properties, prescribing it mixed with wine for curative effect. By royal edict, physicians were advised to utilize the gall and the liver of the pig in prescriptions, and lard was recommended as well.

Osiris, an Egyptian god, supposedly was killed by a boar. Osiris cults that focused on the theme of resurrection spread throughout the Mediterranean world and were especially vital during the Roman Empire. Pigs were sacrificed to Osiris each year on his birthday. Pigs were also sacrificed when the moon was full (perhaps encouraging today's superstition that hogs must be slaughtered when the moon is full or the meat will shrink when cooked) and on certain other feast days. Only men were allowed to participate and, due to edicts from their priests, that was the only time the men were allowed to eat pork.

The Pig in Judaism

Jews were not allowed to kill pigs, offer pigs for sacrifice, or even touch the carcass of a dead pig for Levitical code denounced the use of swine's flesh as a breach of the law and an abomination in the sight of the Lord. The ancient Hebrews would not even speak the word for swine; they referred to the animal as "that beast" or "that thing." This passage from the Old Testament holds the pig in abomination, as described in Leviticus 11:7:

And the Lord said to Moses and Aaron, "Say to the people of Israel, These are the living things which you may eat among all the beasts that are on the earth. Whatever parts the hoof and is cloven-footed and chews the cud, among the animals, you may eat. Nevertheless among those that chew the cud or part the hoof, you shall not eat these. . . . And the swine, because it parts the hoof and is cloven-footed but does not chew the cud, is unclean to you. Of their flesh you shall not eat, and their carcasses you shall not touch; they are unclean to you."

Surely the fact that hogs are excellent scavengers with omnivorous tastes that include human bodily wastes, as well as those excreted from other animals, did not go unnoticed and perpetuated their "unclean" repute.

Some scholars suggest that in addition to the Levitical code Jews abstained from eating pork to avoid the possibility of idolatry. The Sumarians—gentiles who held them in captivity before the days of Abraham—had worshiped and sacrificed

Pigs In Papua New Guinea

An Ice Age land bridge once connected Australia and New Guinea, but that bridge was destroyed about 12,000 years ago, cutting off the mountainous island and isolating it from Australia and the rest of the world. In fact, New Guinea tribes located in tiny villages have warred with one another for 500 generations and today they remain so isolated from one another that almost a thousand languages can be found.

Paupa New Guinea became an Australian territory in 1975. It is a wild place, where cannibalism is practiced and few outside influences prevail. The tribe living in the section known as Kaulong is a pig culture—they believe pigs and humans occupy a single continuum of existence; pigs may behave more or less like humans and humans may behave more or less like pigs. Raising pigs is an important responsibility and pigs are an important symbol of political and social power. At birth, for example, powdered lime is blown into the nostrils of the piglet to make it forget its natural mother and cause it to bond with its human one.

In *Pigs: A Handbook to Breeds of the World* (1993), Valerie Porter explains that pigs are involved in a variety of tribal ceremonies: "They are sacrificed in some places to appease the ancestral spirits and they play central roles at major occasions such as rites of passage (births, the weaning of children, the initiation of boys, a girl's first menstruation, weddings, and funerals) or ventures such as house building and boat building, and in the festivals at which local men of influence match themselves in prestige competitions. They are also exchanged at peacemaking ceremonies after violent disputes."

Porter says the men of the western highlands claim, "Pigs are our hearts!" and "young pigs are treated as pets: they share their owner's cooked food, they are ritually named and baptised, they are given magical treatments for illness, and the women chew up tubers for feeding to weak piglets.

"While the men own the pigs, the role of caring for these precious animals is taken by the women, and with considerable pride. They name their animals, share their sleeping-quarters with them (the men sleep separately), fondle them like any other pet and occasionally suckle orphaned piglets themselves."

The most valuable pig to own is known as a "tusker." According to Jane Goodale's book, *To Sing With Pigs Is Human* (1995), "Some pigs have their upper canines removed, permitting the lower canines to grow unimpeded and perhaps even in a full circle to re-enter the lower jaw, a process that can take ten or twelve years. Specialists are paid handsomely

The pig in Papua New Guinea

There are many "cattle cultures" in the world but very few "pig cultures." In Papua New Guinea, where there are 1.5 million pigs and 3.8 million people, villagers say, "Pigs are our hearts."

for removing the upper canines of these pigs. After this procedure, the owner of a tusker will employ many spells and all-night hamlet ceremonies to enhance the tusker's growth...."

The adult tribal members blacken their own teeth with manganese oxide because white, visible teeth signify aggression (like a pig's tusk). Tusks are made into ornaments, which a man must kill another man to earn permission to wear. When the men of the tribe are challenging others in battle, they clench pigs' tusks between their own teeth to appear more aggressive. This means, Goodale says, "Watch out, I can be like a pig. I am powerful and dangerous."

Jesus and the Swine

References to swine appear throughout the New Testament. In Jesus' parable of the Prodigal Son (Luke 15:11–32) the young man who squandered his inheritance ended up in a place where "a great famine arose in that country and he began to be in want. So he went and joined himself to one of the citizens of that country, who sent him into his fields to feed swine. And he would gladly have fed on the pods that the swine ate; and no one gave him anything." In fact, he soon had enough of this repugnant occupation and went back home to his father who greeted him with open arms and killed the fatted calf.

In the story of the Gadarene swine (Mark 5:8–13), a lunatic possessed of devils pleaded with Christ that the devils be removed, and at his suggestion they were cast into a herd of swine that grazed nearby. Swine were thus assigned a relationship with devils that has been carried through generations and perpetuated through centuries:

> For he said to him, "Come out of the man, you unclean spirit!" And Jesus asked him, "What is your name?" He replied, "My name is Legion for we are many." And he begged him eagerly not to send him out of the country. Now a great herd of swine was feeding there on the hillside; and they begged him, "Send us to the swine, let us enter them." So Jesus gave them leave. And the unclean spirits came out, and entered the swine; and the herd, numbering about two thousand, rushed down the steep bank into the sea, and were drowned in the sea.

"The Prodigal Son Among the Swine"
Pen and ink drawing by Albrecht Dürer, 1498. In the Biblical story of the Prodigal Son, the young man who squandered his inheritance ended up working as a swineherd. "And he would gladly have fed on the pods that the swine ate; and no one gave him anything." In fact, he soon had enough of this repugnant occupation and went back home to his father who greeted him with open arms and killed the fatted calf.

According to Brewer's *Dictionary of Phase and Fable,* there are very small holes in the forefeet of pigs, visible only when the hair has been carefully removed. Tradition says the apertures are where the "legion of devils" entered the Gadarene swine. Around each hole are six rings that look as if they were burned or branded into the skin, and these are supposed to be the marks of the devil's claws.

pigs to their god Baal. To offer that same animal to a Jewish deity would have been an insult, perhaps inviting the anger of their own God.

Beyond hygiene or the common fear that the gross and sensual qualities of the pig were acquired by eating its flesh, the Jews had an abundance of cattle and sheep that provided beef and mutton, so they really had no need of pork. Hogs do not thrive in a hot climate anyway, and pork quickly becomes unwholesome without refrigeration in such a locale.

The Israelites may have avoided pork due to its association with leprosy (perhaps actually trichinosis), which was caused by eating undercooked pork. It is possible that the Hebrew aversion to pork initially grew out of an Egyptian sanitary regulation. One scholar claims that after the Jews settled in Palestine, their scruples did not prevent them from the possibility of poisoning those of other faiths; in Palestine, the Jews raised pigs but fed pork only to the gentiles within their gates.

Jewish lore includes the question posed by Isaiah 66:17, "They that sanctify themselves and purify themselves in the gardens behind one tree in the midst eating swine's flesh and the abomination and the mouse shall be consumed together." This has been interpreted as an inference that pork may have been eaten in secret.

In *The Golden Bough: A Study in Magic and Religion* (1912), anthropologist Sir James George Frazer echoed this suspicion by proposing that the pig was originally revered instead of despised. Until the time of Isaiah, he claimed, "Jews met secretly in gardens to eat the flesh of swine and mice as a religious rite." The tradition was an ancient one, dating from a period when both the pig and mouse were venerated as divine and their flesh was eaten during rare and solemn sacramental occasions as the body and blood of gods.

Throughout the centuries, Jews have been willing to accept martyrdom rather than eat pork. The Spanish Inquisition (1478–1834) was an attempt to seek out and punish converted Jews and Muslims who secretly practiced their original beliefs. Because Jews and Muslims were prohibited from eating pork, a person who refused to eat it was in danger of arrest. Anxious to prove his orthodoxy, Philip II of Spain, who was Catholic, zealously consumed such vast quantities of bacon that he nearly died.

The Pig in Europe

In the countries of central Europe, pigs have traditionally represented good luck and prosperity, in addition to (and puzzlingly so) gluttony, obstinacy, and indolence. Eubuleus—the name of the swineherd who told Demeter the earth had swallowed her daughter and his pigs—means "of good counsel," and in earliest European times swineherds were considered magicians or soothsayers. Sometimes the pigs themselves were credited with prophetic powers.

In northern Europe, one served pork as an indication of hospitality. Both the Anglo-Saxons and the conquering Norman aristocrats enjoyed pork; evidence of the popularity of pork appeared among all English classes in the past. But pork, taboo to Jews and Moslems, was unwelcome in Scotland and parts of northern

"As a jewel of gold in a swine's snout, so is a fair woman which is without discretion."
—Proverbs 11:22

37

Hog

This hog portrait is from the eighteenth-century *Histoire Naturelle* by George Louis Leclerc, *comte de Buffon*, a French scientist appointed by Louis XV to catalog the animals in the king's museum. This beast possesses a rather sinister appearance, not unusual in depictions of pigs, for their relationship with devils has perpetuated since the Biblical story of the Gadarine Swine.

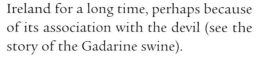

Ireland for a long time, perhaps because of its association with the devil (see the story of the Gadarine swine).

William the Conqueror ordered the creation of the Doomsday Book in 1085 and 1086, a census listing English landowners and their property, including their pigs. Records indicate the domestic pig population in the counties of Norfolk, Sussex, and Essex totaled more than thirty-one thousand.

During the time of history known as the Iron Age, Ireland was called Muicinis, or "Pig Island," but the word "pig" was not even uttered in Scotland, for the word itself brought bad luck. In her 1940 book *English Folklore*, Christina Hole affirms that, "In the Highlands . . . sailors and fishermen rarely mention the animal by its proper name, but refer to it by some term of their own. . . . To meet a pig on the way to the boat is very unlucky."

In northern Europe, chieftains feasted on pork. After death, warriors purportedly enjoyed meals of pork in Valhalla, and the Celts buried pigs' bones and joints of pork with the dead. The ancient European corn spirit appeared in the form of a pig.

Pigs are frequently represented in European Books of Hours—especially Books of Hours of the Virgin Mary, or psalters—which contained a prescribed order of prayers and readings from scripture for certain periods of time. September utilized illustrations that associated the month with the boar hunt. The month of October frequently represented the month of porculatio, or "fattening of the swine," the time when pigs were driven into the woods to be fattened on acorns. Many colorful paintings depict the swineherd or peasants knocking acorns from the oak trees for their swine. November (known as *Slaghtmonat* in Old German) was the month for slaughtering hogs in preparation for Christmas feasts.

"Do not give what is holy to dogs—they will only turn and attack you. Do not throw your pearls in front of swine—they will only trample them underfoot."
—From the Sermon on the Mount, Matthew 7:6

**Nineteenth-century woodcut of swine-
herd with swine**
This idyllic setting belies the contempt with
which the position of swineherd was traditionally regarded.

The Swine Chronicles

Paleocene/Eocene Epochs (37–65 million years ago): The dinosaurs have disappeared, and a variety of mammals begin to emerge as the oceans recede. Primitive ancestors of the pig appear in Eocene and middle Miocene formations in Europe, India, and America.

Oligocene Epoch (23–37 million years ago): About 36 million years ago, the pig family plants its roots with the giant hog known as *Elotherium*, or *Entelodont*, a fierce, omnivorous creature as large as a cow or sometimes as big as a bison. During the Oligocene epoch two distinct branches of the piglike family emerge: the peccaries, which still exist in the southwest United States and South America, and the Old World pigs that continued to develop in Africa and Eurasia. The Old World wild boar is thought to be the direct ancestor of all the varieties of our domestic pig.

95,000–90,000 B.C.: Fossils of the first true humans, *Homosapiens*, date back to this period in time.

35,000–20,000 B.C.: Cave paintings of boars and other sacred animals are created by Ice Age artists in caves located at Altamira, Spain and Lascaux, France.

7000 B.C.: In his scholarly work, *Origin of Species* (1859), Charles Darwin suggests pigs were domesticated in China at this time. Other estimates date Chinese hog domestication several thousand years earlier, circa 9000 B.C.

3486 B.C.: Emperor Fo-Hi of China decrees that swine should be bred and raised in this country and encourages the import of domestic hogs from the west.

3000 B.C.: Immigrant pigs are found in Sweden. These pigs are smaller than the wild boar and show no signs of having been bred from or with it.

1165 B.C.: According to Virgil, it was around this time that Aeneas experienced his vision of the Sacred White Sow that determined the City of Rome should be built on the Tiber River.

1122 B.C.–221 B.C.: During China's Chou Dynasty, tiny clay models of pigs are placed in the hands of the dead at burial so that their pigs would accompany them into the afterlife.

863 B.C.: The medicinal properties of the waters at Bath, England, are discovered by Prince Baldred, eldest son of Hudibras, a British king. Baldred, ill with leprosy, was working as a swineherd in a remote and untraveled part of his father's country. One day his pigs got away from him and ran into the mud at the hot springs of Bath. He noticed that when they emerged from the mud their skin was smooth and unblemished, and he wondered if the springs would heal his skin disease as well. They did, and the cured prince returned to his father and reported the spings' healing properties. A statue of King Baldred (for he eventually became king) was erected on that spot in 1699. The pigs and the service they provided have yet to be recognized.

621 B.C.: The Old Testament book of Deuteronomy is written, and the taboos against pork become part of the dietary restrictions among Jews.

471 B.C.: Around this time, Buddha calls all the animals to come to him, and the pig (or wild boar) ends up in twelfth place, ensuring his position representing the twelfth year in the Chinese calendar.

60 B.C.: Coins depicting winged boars and small pigs had been minted in Rhodes and Sicily prior to this time, but in 60 B.C. the Roman *denarius*, the silver coin of the Roman Empire, illustrates a wild boar being attacked by a hound.

13 B.C.: In his *Odes*, Horace (Quintus Horatius Flaccus) writes, "Think to yourself that every day is your last; the hour to which you do not look forward will come as a welcome surprise. As for me, when you want a good laugh, you will find me, in a fine state, flat and sleek, a true hog of Epicurious' herd."

A.D. 77: Pliny, the Roman historian, eloquently expresses his declaration that pork contains at least fifty different flavors.

A.D. 140: The *sestertius* is minted at the decree of Roman Emperor Antoninus Pius. It features the Great Sow and Piglets, commemorating the legend of the founding of Rome by Aeneas (see 1165 B.C.).

A.D. 356: Saint Anthony of Egypt, patron saint of swine and swineherds, dies (see chapter 3).

A.D. 625: Mohammed forbids his followers to consume pork.

A.D. 900: During the tenth century, Howel Dha, the law giver of Wales, decreed that the various values of hogs were to be determined as follows (Latin translation by Wotton in his *Leges Wallicie*, 1841): "The price of a little pig from the time it is born until it grows to burrow, is one penny; when it ceases sucking, which is at the end of three months, it is worth two pence; from that time it goes to the wood with the swine, and it is considered as a swine, and its value is four pence; from the Feast of St. John unto the 1st day of January, its value is fifteen pence; from the 1st of January unto the Feast of St. John, its value is twenty-four pence; and from that time forward its value shall be thirty pence, the same as its mother."

1132: Crown Prince Louis Philippe, heir to the French throne, suffers a fatal accident when his horse trips over a pig, while riding through the streets of Paris.

1066: On October 14, the Battle of Hastings is completed, marking the Norman conquest of England by William the Conqueror, Duke of Normandy. This results in the adoption of the French words *porc, boeuf, mouton, veau,* and *poulard,* as the basis of the English words "pork," "beef," "mutton," "veal," and "poultry."

1080: William the Conqueror orders the Doomsday Book, a written census surveying English landowners and their property, to be compiled. The pig populations of Norfolk, Sussex, and Essex combined total more than 31,000 domestic pigs.

1300: Pigs are now the most popular livestock animal in Europe, and depictions of pigs are used in advertisements for the benefit of people who cannot read the words for "Butcher Shop."

1457: A sow and her six piglets are tried on charges of murdering and partially devouring a child in the French town of Savigny-sur-tang. A guilty sentence is handed down for the sow, who is subsequently put to death, but mercy is extended to the piglets, who are released due to their youth and immaturity.

1478: This year marks the beginning of the Spanish Inquisition (1478–1834), established by the monarchy to uncover and punish Jews and Muslims who secretly practiced their own religions. A distaste for pork is a test of heresy.

1483: Richard III seizes the throne of England. His nickname is "The Hog" and his coat of arms contains the wild boar.

1493–1496: Queen Isabella of Spain insists that explorer Christopher Columbus carry eight specially selected hogs on his second voyage across the Atlantic Ocean to the New World. The pigs are deposited on the shores of Haiti but are eventually transported to North America.

1533: Catherine de' Medici, wife of Henry II of France, expresses her fondness for truffles. The French train dogs and pigs to sniff for these exotic delicacies.

1539: Hernando de Soto introduces the first pigs to North America, bringing them to the Florida mainland.

1643: Hungarian archbishop György Szelepcsény reports, "In every farm of mine I keep animals of a different colour, in one the

blond ones, in another the piebald, the black and white or spotted ones, and again in another the black ones," indicating selection for color is one of the currently accepted steps in creating and consolidating a breed.

1776–1777: Salt pork smuggled behind enemy lines to Valley Forge becomes the staple fare of soldiers under the command of General George Washington in the Revolutionary War.

1830: British journalist William Cobbett writes of the cure for the deterioration of rural life in England in his *Rural Rides*: "A pig in almost every cottage sty! That is the infallible mark of happy people!"

1863: Cincinnati, Ohio, has become a major pork processing center and is nicknamed "Porkopolis." This handle lasts only a short while, however, due to the Civil War, which interferes with access to the city. After the war Chicago becomes known as the world's largest pork packing center or "Hog Butcher to the World."

1870: The invention of the refrigerated railroad car makes it possible to ship fresh pork long distances without salting or smoking it prior to shipment.

1906: The very first (albeit unsuccessful) pig-to-human transplant occurs, as a French surgeon connects a pig's kidney to the malfunctioning kidney of a woman.

1922: Insulin is commercially extracted from a pig's pancreas and used to control diabetes.

1950: It is discovered that Henry County, Illinois, produces more hogs than any other county in the United States, so the first official "Hog Festival" is celebrated in the city of Kewanee.

1971: The first pig heart valve is transplanted into a human recipient.

1976: Swine flu is predicted to sweep the United States and the nation is innoculated against the disease. Only 6 documented cases appear, but 535 of those receiving innoculations develop

Guillain-Barre Syndrome.

1998: The pork industry suffers a major setback as hog prices stand at their lowest level since the Depression. The crisis is blamed on huge corporate hog operations that glut slaughterhouses and leave smaller farmers facing financial ruin. As a result, from 1997 to 1998, farmers receive 39 percent less for sales of pork. But the percentage decline in the price consumers pay is only 1.5 percent.

1998: Bert and Ernie, two pigs taught by Penn State University Professor Stanley Curtis, develop a fondness for electronic technology when they learn to relay their thoughts to humans using icons on a computer screen, respond to voice commands, and manipulate controls in their room to regulate the temperature. After their retirement, the pigs relaxed at a pig sanctuary. Dale Riffle, sanctuary director, said Bert and Ernie "contributed greatly to educating the world that pigs are not stupid, unfeeling creatures. They are true ambassadors for advancing the humane treatment of animals typically used for food production."

1999: Xenotransplantation, or the transplant of a variety of pig organs, becomes more than a theoretical possibility. Pigs are favored because the size of their organs is about the size of those in humans; pigs have relatively short gestation periods and produce large litters, thus providing a generous supply of potential organ donors. The most promising approach to widespread Xenotransplantation now lies in the genetic engineering of pigs so that their organs will not be recognized as "foreign." To achieve this, Xenotransplant researchers are developing ways to add specific human genes to fertilized pig eggs.

Chapter 2

The Wild Boar in the Wood

There is a wild boar in the wood
And he eats men's bones and he
drinks their blood

Old Baggum, he took his wooden knife
And he swore, by God, he'd take its life.

Old Baggum, he rode to the
wild boar's den
And he spied the bones of a
thousand men. . . .

—Howie Mitchell, a version of *Old Bangum* (or *Old Baggum* or *Wild Hog in the Woods*), one of many variations of the old folksong, "Sir Lionel," taken from the Arthurian legend

"This foul, grim, urchin-snouted boar . . ."
Facing page: This foul, grim, urchin-snouted boar . . .
His snout digs sepulchres where'er he goes;
Being mov'd, he strikes whate'er is in his way,
And whom he strikes his cruel tushes slay.
—*Venus and Adonis*, William Shakespeare (1593) (Photograph © Craig Blacklock)

Wild boar on armorial shield
Inset: From the sixteenth-century manuscript, *Prince Arthur's Book*.

Compared to the cow, sheep, and horse, the pig may be today's most primitive domestic mammal. The chronicle of the domestic pig is inextricably tied to that of its wild ancestor, the wild boar, which was greatly admired and even worshiped for its courage and ferocity. The wild boar, *Sus scrofa*, is the largest of all the wild pigs and is distinguished most notably from our domesticated pig by its tusks, which it uses as weapons. The tusks are actually canine teeth that are curved and prismlike in shape, two of which jut from the upper jaw and two even larger that come out of the lower jaw. The boar sharpens its lower tusks by rubbing them against the upper tusks. These enable the boar to inflict terrible wounds by ripping in an upward direction and aiming at the soft parts of other animals, such as the flanks, belly, or groin. As the boar grows older, the lower tusks eventually curve inward and upward over the snout until they are useless for attack, although they provide some defense in fights with other boars during the rutting season. At the same time, the upper tusks develop outward and upward, providing alternative weapons of offense.

> The natural life span of a pig is fifteen to twenty years. Wild boars, if free from predators, sometimes last twenty-five.

In 1853, David Low described the wild boar in his book, *On the Domesticated Animals of the British Islands*: "There is something noble in the courage of this powerful and solitary creature," he said. "All his strength seems to be given him for self-defense. He injures no one, unless when disturbed in his retreat, or in search of the food which his nature leads him to seek. He does not court a combat with enemies that thirst for his blood, but for the most part he seeks to secure himself by betaking himself to the nearest covert. If attacked by savage dogs . . . he rushes upon the foremost and strongest, maiming and killing numbers of the pack . . . when wearied and tormented and forced at length to fight for his life, he turns on his persecutors and aims at vengeance."

The Celebrated Boar

The boar was viewed as a curious representation of both fertility and destruction. He was the most dangerous quarry for the hunter, symbolizing death and carnage; the boar was an incarnation of evil, an embodiment of the dead. Conversely, the boar was also a symbol of fertility and an emblem of courage and ferocity. These conflicting representations encouraged the boar's role in folklore and legend. The boar became entwined in superstition and in turn was detested, feared, worshiped and sacrificed, venerated, and vilified.

Despite the presence of domesticated swine, numerous religious myths from ancient times share a common bond: The god in question was killed by a wild boar or by an enemy whose symbol was the wild boar. As a result, gods, goddesses, and other divine beings were frequently associated with swine. In Egypt, for example, the evil god Set was porcine in form. Traces of a similar concept in the West can be found in the story of King Arthur's boar-hunt, in which the fabulous boar is the emissary of Satan, to be overcome not by force but by prayer.

The powerful and mysterious boar eventually came to be invoked by soothsayers, magicians, wizards, priests, and medicine men. Boars' tusks and hooves have traditionally been used as amulets and other magical ornamentation. An infusion of boar's tusk was thought to cure epilepsy, toothache, and a variety of other ailments including "the twinges." For generations, soothsayers and medicine men have invoked the aid of swine

The Swine Family Tree

Order: *Artiodactyla*
Suborder: *Suiformes*
Infraorder: *Suina*
Family: *Suidae*
Subfamily: *Suinae*
Potamochoerus (African river hogs and bush pigs)
Sus (Wild boar of Europe and India and domestic pigs)
Phacochoerus (African wart hogs)
Hylochoerus (African forest hogs)
Babirussa (Tusked hog of the Celebes)
Porcula (Pigmy hogs of the Himalayas)
Family: *Tayassuidae* or *Dictoylidae*
Tayassu (Peccaries or javelinas)
Dicotyles tayassu (collared peccary, North and South America)
Dicotyles labiatus (white-lipped peccary, South America)
Infraorder: *Ancodonta*
Family: *Hippopotamidae* (the "river horse" of Africa is a distant relative)

Swine family tree
Chromolithograph from *Johnson's Household Book of Nature* (1880).

The jungles of South America are full of large herds of wild pigs, which, in bulk, are the most dangerous animals in the wild. They are quite fearless, and by reason of their numbers can pull down anything in their path.
—Julian Duguid, *Green Hell* (1931)

Wild boar in heraldry
Examples of wild boar in European heraldry, as shown in coat of arms and similar bookplate belonging to Captain Georges C. Swinton. Swinton may have chosen the emblem of the boar as a play on words ("Swine-ton").

Domestic wild boar
Domestic wild boar raised at Black Creek Wild Boar Farm, Ontario, Canada. (Photograph © Dave Kubassek/Black Creek Wild Boar)

by utilizing their fresh livers as mirrors through which to discern the future, because the liver was the seat of the soul and reflected the divine rays sent down by the gods.

In Mycenean Greece, warriors wore helmets shaped in the form of a boar's head or fastened ornaments of boar's tusks or boar's teeth on their shields or helmets, according to Homer. The boar was sacred to Ares (or Mars), the god of war, destruction, and strife. It was commonly believed that by carrying an image of the boar's head, you were saved from danger and granted the boar's life-force and vitality to guide you through battle, for the boar was the slayer of men and of gods.

There were few animals more important to the Celts than the boar. The boar was sacred to the Celtic Goddess Arduinna, patroness of the forests of the Ardennes. Boar's blood was felt to beget gods back in primitive times when it was believed that blood generated offspring. Bones of boars were used in burial rituals and found in graves of the Celts. Figures of boars appear on ancient British and Irish altars. Irish myths contain divine, magical, and prophetic boars, supernatural and otherworldly pigs who cause death and disaster. The Druids called themselves boars, existing as solitary beings in the forest as the boars lived.

The boar symbol was prevalent in pre-Christian Europe, and the use of the *sanglier*, or boar emblem, in European heraldry may be traced back to this origin. In 1483, Richard III took the English throne and was nicknamed "The Hog" in response to the wild boar on his coat of arms. An English landowner, William

Collingbourne, wrote that "The Cat, the Rat, and Lovell our dog / Rule all England under a hog," in reference to others who were subject to Richard III's rule. (Collingbourne was eventually executed on Tower Hill for conspiracy against the king). But in 1485, when Henry VII defeated and killed Richard III at Bosworth Field, ending the Wars of the Roses, many innkeepers scurried to repaint the white boar on their signs blue, the Earl of Oxford's color. Pubs known as the Blue Boar still exist in England today.

In Norman sculpture, the boar is sometimes used to symbolize the forces of evil that are opposed to Christianity, such as the wild beast of the eighth Psalm that roots up the tree of life: "Thou didst bring a vine out of Egypt; thou didst drive out the nations and plant it. Thou didst clear the ground for it; it took deep root and filled the land. . . . The boar from the forest ravages it, and all that move in the field feed on it."

A wild boar was also the emblem of the Roman Twentieth Legion, and stone models of this boar found near the Roman Wall in Britain are similar to the Altamira cave paintings. Other primitive rock paintings of boars may be seen in Southern Rhodesia. Near Dunadd, Argyllshire, Scotland, where ancient Scottish kings were crowned, there are primitive carvings of boars.

Bagging the Wild Boar

Cro-Magnon sketches of wild boars illustrate French caves, and paintings of pigs created by cave-dwellers at Altamira in Spain have been carbon dated at 13,500 B.C.

Centuries before the birth of Christ,

Cave drawing
Facsimile of a wild boar cave drawing at Altamira, Spain (circa 13,500 B.C.). It is thought that the image of a wild boar leaping to attack was created as part of a Paleolithic ritual to give the hunters power over the hunted.

The *sow* was a British term sometimes given to the last sheaf of harvest wheat, which was saved and used to form a loaf of bread in the form of a boar. This loaf was kept on the Yule table until the festivities were completed, and afterward it was held until the spring sowing, at which time part of it would be eaten and the rest mixed with the seed corn to promise a healthy crop.

European wild boar

Illustration from Buffon's *Historie Naturelle* (1766). Because of ancient religious myths, the boar became entwined in superstition and was, in turn, detested, feared, worshiped and sacrificed, venerated and vilified. The powerful and mysterious boar eventually came to be invoked by soothsayers, magicians, wizards, priests, and medicine men.

Homer recorded the first account of a boar hunt in the *Iliad* XIII:

> As when a mountain boar,
> Bold in his might, abides the on-
>   coming rout,
> In lonely spot—bristles his ridgy
>   back,
> His eyes blaze fire, his tusks he
>   whets the while,
> All eager to beat back both dogs and
>   men. . . .

Marco Polo reported on boar hunting exploits in China during the thirteenth century. The Emperor Kublai Khan left the capital for Mongolia in March of each year with cheetahs (which he called hunting leopards) trained to catch boars and wild cattle. The Mongols and the Manchus continued to hunt boars with spears for four hundred years after the development of firearms.

The wild boar was abundant during the Middle Ages, found mostly in France, Germany, and Britain. Due to the beast's ferocity and cunning, hunting wild boar was a popular pursuit for British nobility and male members of the royal family. But by the time of William the Conqueror (1027–1087), wild boar had become so scarce that anyone found guilty of killing a wild boar was threatened to have their eyes put out, according to decree.

During the twelfth century, boar remained plentiful in the forests around London. In the first decade of the fifteenth century, Edward, second Duke of York, described the wild boar in his publication *Master of Game,* claiming the animal "is a proud beast and fierce and perilous . . . for some men have seen him slit a man from knee up to the breast and slay him all stark dead at one stroke so that he never spake thereafter."

The exploits of the legendary King Arthur included daring and heroic hunts for wild boar. One tale recited by mediaeval Welsh bards describes the tragic plight of two lovers, forbidden to marry until the proposed groom performed a number of impossible feats, which included the capture of a ferocious wild boar. The frantic groom prevailed upon his cousin, King Arthur, to come to his aid. Arthur recruited his followers, and after months of searching the savage boar was located in Ireland. A pursuit ensued that lasted for months, during which time the boar "laid waste the fifth part of Ireland," say the authors of *Pigs: From Cave to Cornbelt.* The fight continued until the boar ended up in Wales where he "laid low men, cattle, and crops like chaff before a hurricane. Six times he was brought to bay; six times he killed half the attackers and most of the dogs." Eventually he was driven into Cornwall, where the boar ran into the ocean and was never seen again.

Masculine as the act may have been portrayed, bagging the wild boar was not the exclusive pursuit of males. Princess Anne, daughter of Louis XI of France, was fond of hunting both wolves and wild boar. Diane of Poitiers accompanied French King Francis I in encounters with boars and stags.

In the Louvre, in Paris, the Belles Chasses tapestries were commissioned by Margaret of Austria during the sixteenth century. Margaret was a composer of Renaissance music and an unusually

influential woman regarding the politics of the day. She also enjoyed the pastime of boar hunting, for which she dressed in scarlet and green and rode a white horse. Ever the doting daughter, Margaret asked Bernard van Orlay to design the priceless Belles Chasses tapestries, one of which features her father, Maximilian I, Holy Roman emperor and German king, slaying a wild boar singlehandedly with his sword.

Queen Isabella of Spain (yes, *that* Queen Isabella) was apparently a tough woman who interspersed boar hunts with military campaigns. "Days in the saddle made her hard, straight, resourceful, fearless, indifferent to fatigue, contemptuous of pain," wrote Lady Viola Bathurst Apsley, in *Bridleways Through History* (1936). "She became a skillful huntress, commencing with hares and deer but later following the black wild boar, and on one occasion slaying a good-sized boar with her javelin." She was thought to be responsible for the inclusion of pigs among the livestock destined for Cuba during Columbus's second voyage, pigs that eventually ended up

"The next glorious chase"
Pledge me next the glorious chase
When the mighty boars ahead,
He, the noblest of the race,
In the mountain jungle bred
Swifter than the slender deer,
Bounding over Deccan's plain
Who can stay his proud career
Who can hope his tusks to gain?
—Traditional
The frontispiece from *Modern Pig Sticking* (1914),
by Sir Alexander Ernest Wardrop, et al.

sustaining de Soto and other explorers during their ventures into the New World. The descendants of those pigs are still rooting around America today.

Most assuredly, one's conquest of the wild boar earned respect and acclaim. Homer's Odysseus killed a wild boar with a well-aimed spear, but Hercules was the only one to take down a boar with his bare hands. The Etruscans claimed they captured wild boars by the magic of their music, placing their best flute player at the head of the boar-beaters (apparently the flute music lured the wild boar and his sow up to the snares). Pliny the Younger (A.D. 62–133) wrote to Tacitus to say he had captured "three noble boars" with nets. Mastiffs were some-times used to corner wild boar, and they were outfitted with quilted coats, spiked collars, and leather guards to prevent the boar's tusks and hooves from causing injury.

Horace wrote of hunting wild boar in winter with the aid of hounds:

When rain and snows appear,
And wint'ry Jove loud thunders o'er
  the year,
With hounds he drives into the toils
The foaming boar.

Wild boar are still hunted in many countries around the world, including India, where men hunt with horses and spears. Dogs are used for hunting in the southwestern United States (California, Texas, Nevada, Arizona). Hawaii also has a thriving wild boar hunt, as does the region around the Ozark mountains. How's this for a new and different vacation? You can sign up for a guided wild boar hunt in Russia, France, Turkey, Australia, or New Zealand.

The Boar's Head . . . and Don't Forget the Mustard

Norse and Anglo-Saxon invaders carried their own customs along with them to England, including the offering of a boar to the god Freyr and a sow to the Goddess Freyja at the Winter Solstice celebration. The boar was a symbol of the fertility of the land. This custom survived in Old England with the tradition of serving a wild boar's head at Christmas. The apple in the boar's mouth represented the charmed apple of immortality. One of the first recorded mentions of this festivity was in 1170 when, upon the crowning of

Wild Boar: The Other White Meat

In recent years wild boar have been raised for marketing to restaurants and butchers. Wild boar meat, or *cinghiale* in Italian, is a popular meat in Tuscany, where you can find wild boar sausages, wild boar steaks, sliced boar sandwiches, cured boar hams, and ground boar meat in the sauce poured over your pasta. Restaurants and markets advertise their specialization in wild boar.

The wild boar industry in Canada is a relatively new enterprise and a much riskier business than the production of beef or pork. Breeding stock has been imported from Europe to establish Canadian herds. Regional associations of producers have formed the Wild Boar Federation of Canada/ Federation des Eleveurs de Sanglier du Canada.

The meat of the wild boar is lean and dark red, low in cholesterol. An appetite for wild boar meat is beginning to flourish in Saskatchewan and the rest of Canada, as well as in the United States and international markets such as Japan, France, Germany, the United Kingdom, and areas of the Pacific Rim.

The terms "full blood" and "standard" are used to describe the breeding of wild boar. Full bloods have no domestic pig in their background and are therefore considered pure; they are sold at a higher price than standard stock. Standard wild boar may meet the physical requirements for wild boar but may have some percentage of domestic pig. The Wild Boar Federation of Canada is working toward the development of a breed registry and the establishment of breeding stock standards so "full bloods" can be registered, and a uniform, high quality product can be assured.

Wild herd

Above: Wild boar have very coarse bristles with a woolly undercoat and a marked crest along the back. The sows will have eight to fourteen teats with an average of at least twelve. (Photograph © Craig Blacklock)

Wild sow and young

Left: The wild sow might produce only three or four offspring in her first litter, but then in succeeding litters she could give birth to as many as fifteen piglets at a time. Because they can start reproducing so young and have so many piglets in a single litter, the number of a sow's direct descendants can increase exponentially. If she survived threats from hunters and natural predators, she could live (and produce) for up to twenty-five years, which is about the maximum life span. It is theoretically possible, therefore, for a sow to live to see approximately seven million offspring—from children to great-great-great-great-great grandchildren—during her lifetime. (Photograph © Dave Kubassek/Black Creek Wild Boar)

Wild boar in the woods
Right: Wild boar in the woods of Black Creek Wild Boar Farm, Ontario, Canada. Raising wild boar for meat, and, to a lesser extent, breeding stock, is a relatively new industry for Canada. Commercial hunt farms also invite hunters to pay a fee to hunt a wild boar that has been released in a secure area. In addition, markets exist for wild boar by-products such as tusks, bristles, and hide. (Photograph © Dave Kubassek/Black Creek Wild Boar)

Wild boar piglet, with typical striped coloration.
All wild boar piglets are dark brown with pale longitudinal stripes, making them look like very large chipmunks. After three or four months the stripes disappear completely. This striped coloration is not found in domestic pigs anywhere, only in wild pigs, although it has been suggested that these markings remain dormant in domestic pigs and eventually reappear in their young within a couple generations when any of them become feral. This was, in fact, witnessed in the early 1900s in Jamaica and Colombia, South America.

his son, trumpeters led the way to his young son's table after which King Henry II conveyed the ceremonial boar's head.

Some scholars feel the inclusion of the boar's head in the Yuletide festival was a way to replace the pagan winter feast of Yule with Christian celebrations. In *The Book of Christmas* (1837), Thomas K. Hervey describes the boar's head ceremony: "At St. John's, Oxford, in 1607, before the bearer of the boar's head—who was selected for his height and lustiness, and wore a green silk scarf with an empty sword scabbard dangling at his side—went a runner, dressed in a horse-man's coat, having a boar's spear in his hand—a huntsman in green, carrying the naked and bloody sword belonging to the head-bearer's scabbard—and two pages in 'tafatye and sarcenet,' each with a 'mess of mustard.'"

According to William Youatt, author of *The Pig* (1847), "Throughout the whole of England the boar's head was formerly a standard Christmas dish, served with many ceremonies, and ushered in by an ancient chorus chanted by all present, the words of which are preserved in Ritson's Ancient Song:

> The bore's heed in hand bring I
> With "garlands" gay and rosemary
> I pray you all synge merily,
>   Qui estis in convivio.
> The bore's heed, I understande,
> Is the "chefe" servyce in the lande
> Loke where ever it be founde,
>   Servite cum cantico.
> Be gladde, lordes, bothe more and lasse,
> For this hath ordeyned our stewarde,
> To chere you all this Christmasse,
> The bore's heed with mustarde.

Youatt also notes that each Christmas, in

a thoughtful gesture, "the abbot of St. Germain, in Yorkshire, was bound to send yearly a present of a boar's head to the hangman, which a monk was obliged to carry on his own. This rent was paid yearly, at the feast of St. Vincent, the patron of the Benedictines, and on that day the executioner took precedence in the procession of monks."

The Wild Boar in the Wood

On his second journey to the New World, Christopher Columbus took eight selected pigs, according to Bartolome las Casa, missionary historian of the discovery of America. As Richard Lewinsohn noted in *Animals, Men and Myths* (1954), "From the increase of these eight pigs have come the pigs found everywhere today in the lands of the Indies, all which ever were there and ever will be, which have been and still are endless." Columbus reported by letter to His Most Catholic Majesty Queen Isabella regarding the native pigs he had found in the New World—peccaries he came across in Jamaica in 1503. He said they were wild members of the pig family with large misshapen heads.

Wild boar are considered nocturnal omnivores. Their original range was in Eurasia and North Africa, although native populations eventually expanded to include areas from Ireland to Japan, from Egypt to Scandinavia and Siberia. In England, free-roaming wild boar have recently been found in Kent, East Sussex, and Dorset; these animals escaped from farms where they were being bred for meat and are now doing quite well on their own since they have no natural predators.

All European and Asian wild boar are from the same species, *sus scrofa*, and their tails are straight, not curled. They interbreed successfully with each other and also with the domestic pig.

Today's pure wild boar stands around 24 inches (60 cm) at the shoulder and can weigh up to 400 pounds. It is grayish brown, rugged, and sinewy, with a wedge-shaped head and wedge-shaped body. Sharp tusks up to a foot long jut upward from its jaws. It has a straight tail, erect "prick" ears, a nose length of at least 9 inches (22 cm) measured from the tip of the nose to the inside of the eye.

One particular characteristic is the tendency of females and their young to form matriarchal groups known as "sounders" or "drifts." The male wild boars live alone or exist in small groups and only join the females for a short period during the breeding season during the late days of autumn and spring. As with domestic pigs, the gestation is three months, three weeks, and three days, and gilts can breed as young as six months of age.

A wild sow scrapes a hole in the ground to prepare a nest prior to farrowing. She covers the hole with sticks or grass and after farrowing the sow will be extremely protective of her young. Intruders beware!

When they are in herds they can be fairly easily located . . . as the noise they make when feeding is considerable, but a lone pig will lift his snout to listen and sniff the air intently every few minutes. . . .
After his first fright the pig usually stops, and there is a loud blowing noise as he clears his nostrils the better to catch the scent.
—F. Spencer Chapman,
The Jungle is Neutral (1949)

The sacred boar
Wild boars are still thought to retain magical powers and potency in many parts of the world today.

Fairy Pigs, Demon Swine: Folktales, Superstitions, and Saints

Boar of courage, Earth Lord guide,
Protect me always. Be at my side.
—D. J. Conway, *Animal Magick* (1996)

Ouch!
Facing page: The squeal of a pig can reach as high as 115 decibels, three decibels higher than the sound produced by a supersonic Concorde! (Photograph © Lynn M. Stone)

Pigs and four-leaf clover
Inset: In the early twentieth century, a proliferation of porcine imagery appeared on postcards. The pig's rotund body represented cheerfulness and jolly good humor. This 1905 card brings wishes "To be on the pig's back," which signifies prosperity.

Superstitions concerning swine and pork were prevalent in ancient Egypt, where the pig was considered evil most of the time. When seed was sown, however, pigs were permitted to walk over the fields and trample seeds into the fertile soil. Similarly, as the pig began to seek his fortune around the world, the animal internationally influenced a variety of conflicting myths and legends. For example, a carving on the island of Malta illustrates the connection between the sow and the moon: The engraving depicts a sow with thirteen teats, representing the thirteen lunar months of a Goddess Year.

Romans offered sacrificial pigs to their own gods and goddesses: Mars, Ceres, Tellus Mater, and Proserpina. Drinking or washing in pig's blood was an act of purification—a belief repeated in many lands to this day. To Romans, the cowrie shell looked like a little white sow, so they called it *porcella*, or "little sow," from which our word "porcelain" is derived.

55

Tout est bon dans le cochon! This is a rural French expression, meaning "All of the pig—from head to tail—is good." It is associated with the "Fete du Cochon," a Sunday ritual gathering of family and friends following the slaughter of a pig, where every dish of the meal will contain some part of the pig.

In some parts of the world, however, it is felt that even speaking the word "pig" is an invitation to grief. Therefore, a similar word with a more beneficent meaning may be used to placate malignant spirits; the name "pig" is avoided and the creature is referred to as the "short-legged" or the "grunting animal" or even "the beautiful one." A peculiar phrase to avoid the direct term "pig" is found in some parts of China, where it is known as "the long-nosed general."

United Kingdom

In Great Britain, boars symbolize courage and the strength of warriors for they are strong, dangerous, and difficult to kill. When boars appear in dreams and visions they represent warriors. Isolt's premonition of Tristan's death came about when she dreamed of the death of a great boar. Statues of boars are occasionally found in the vicinity of statues of armed warriors, indicating an association between the two.

There is much importance accorded to the bristles of the boar in Welsh folktales. In the story of Culhwch and Olwen, King Arthur fought extraordinary boars with bristles of gold and silver. In Welsh mythology, the theme of the hunt often involved animals that pass between the realm of magic and the gods. King Arthur pursued a "gleaming white boar" in one story, and the boar led him to a magical trap. In another Welsh legend, King Arthur and his men hunted Twrch Trwyth, a king who had been turned into a boar, for a comb and shears, treasures that he carried between his ears.

Cailleach, the Earth Mother, had a pig that attended her and always "took the hindmost in the dance." In Celtic mythology, the boar or pig was considered to be a supernatural being with prognostic powers as well as a harbinger of death and disaster.

Pig bones (in addition to those of horses and cattle) have been found inside ancient Welsh and Celtic graves, indicating their importance to the well-being of people of those cultures where the prosperity of the clan was represented by the prosperity of its herds.

Until the nineteenth century, many country folk believed the devil lived in the mountains of Wales and sometimes appeared as a black pig, although he could assume any form except that of a white sheep. To keep the black pig from entering their homes, people whitewashed their doorsteps. The Black Boar as the personification of Satan carried over into folklore of New England and Ireland. The Black Sow was seen by the Celts as an evil animal symbolizing death, cold, and great evil. Even today in Wales it is believed by some that the Black Pig appears on Halloween.

The White Sow was the personification of the Welsh goddess Cerridwen, a Great Mother and lunar deity. White sows were responsible for the location of Rome, a variety of monasteries, and some churches. Those who were influenced by the vision of the White Sow saw it as a symbol of divine inspiration.

Fairy pigs have been reported emanating from the Isle of Man. A ghost pig has been said to have been seen at Andover in Hampshire on New Year's Eve. During an eclipse in Wales, people imitate the grunting of pigs. It is also felt that the squeal of a pig will dissipate St. Elmo's Fire.

In 1519, it was reported that witches

Get 'em while they're small
Sure, these six Chester White piglets can fit in bushel basket now, but by the time they are six months old, the little piggies will have increased their birth weight by more than 6,000 percent! (Photograph © J. C. Allen & Son, West Lafayette, IN)

Bringing home the bacon
Below: To "bring home the bacon" can mean to succeed in making one's point. It may also be taken literally, such as bringing home the bacon by catching the greased pig at the fair. A 1720 dictionary refers to bacon as "the Prize, of whatever kind which Robbers make in their Enterprizes." And to "save one's bacon" means to escape with the Prize or make a narrow escape.

Ask your Grocer for
SHAW'S Limerick BACON & HAMS.
"A Breakfast Luxury"
As Supplied to Royalty.

Pig pride
Above: A 4-H Club boy in North Carolina proudly displays his Hampshire pig. (Photograph © J. C. Allen & Son Inc., West Lafayette, IN)

in England rode not only cats and goats but also pigs when undertaking their malefic missions. The pig was considered extremely vulnerable to the Evil Eye, so therefore it was not to be trusted. English peasants were familiar with demon pigs. The Winwick and Burnley pigs of Lancashire were the most well known, and their effigies are carved on the walls of parish churches. In Lincolnshire, the custom arose of scoring the back of a living pig with a red-hot poker to preserve the remainder of the litter.

Scotland has always treated the pig with disfavor and has considered it very unlucky for a pig to cross your path, especially if you're a fisherman. The very mention of the word "pig" was believed to bring disaster that could be averted by cold iron, the only charm strong enough to keep evil spirits away. In their book *The Symbolic Pig* (1961), F. C. Sillar and R. M. Meyler note that it was considered especially "unlucky to refer to swine by name while at sea, more especially when baiting the lines, and even in the safety of church, tough fishermen would feel for the nails in their boots and whisper 'cauld airn' when the story of the Gadarene swine was read."

Irish folklore has many references to pigs. *Muic-inis*, or "Pig Island," is one of the ancient names for that country. In Ireland, as in Wales, a black pig is a bad sign. However, they believe illness can be averted if you walk around a pigsty three times. If you "hear like a trespassing pig," you can hear really well.

Scandinavia and Europe

In Scandinavian mythology, "Gullinborsti" (meaning "Golden Bristles") was the name of the sacred boar with "terrible tusks" that belonged to Freyr, the fertility god, and in his honor a boar was sacrificed at Yuletide. Northern Germans believed Gullinbursti could reveal secrets and detect lies. Freyr's sister, Freyja, rode a sow named *Hildisvini*, or "Battle Pig." Swedish kings once wore boar masks to indicate their spiritual marriage with this goddess.

The Norse-Teutonic god Heimdall was said to have been fathered by boar's blood. Another mythic Scandinavian boar, Saehrimnir, was killed and eaten fresh every day by the dead heroes who resided in Valhalla.

Germans commonly associated the pig with storms and fertility. In central Germany, it was felt that the corn spirit took the form of the pig, and when the wind would sweep through the barley farmers would say, "The Boar is rushing through the corn."

In some parts of Germany, people ate pea soup with dried pork ribs on Ash Wednesday or Candlemas, after which the ribs were collected and hung in the room until planting time when they were buried in the field or put in a bag containing flaxseed. This was thought to prevent earth fleas and moles from inflecting the flax, allowing a healthy crop.

Estonians called the last sheaf harvested the "Rye-boar," and the man who took it in was greeted with, "You have the Rye-boar on your back!" to which he would reply with a song of prayer for plenty.

Latvians revered the pig at planting time and the pig, representing the corn spirit, was believed to carry special powers in his tail. In certain parts of Latvia,

---

Italian Pig Curses

The Italians have a whole herd of colorful curses related to porkers. Some are simple playful epithets made with porcine prefixes. Others are serious swinish sacrilege that would never, ever be uttered in polite company. In order of increasing severity, here are a handful of prime Italian pig curses:

Porca miseria ("pig misery"; a common, childish lament)
Porca vacca ("pig cow")
Porca puttana or *porca troia* ("pig whore")
Porca Giuda ("pig Judas")
Porca puttana Eva ("pig whore Eve")
Porco dio ("pig God"; *porco zio*, or "pig uncle," is a more polite play on *porco dio*)
Porca Madonna ("pig Madonna"; a serious, blasphemous curse)

"The Squealing Pig" is a pub in County Monaghan, Ireland. The public house itself has stood on that corner for more than a hundred years, but was given its current name in 1991. Regulars refer to it more succinctly as "The Pig."

Porcine Patois, Part One: From Piggy Banks to Piggy Back

 When it comes to defining the multitudinous colloquial references of pig implication, a few clues may be beneficial.

A **pig** is (take your pick):
- another name for a hog
- an earthenware vessel
- a section of an orange
- a sixpenny coin
- a police officer
- a printer or pressman
- a piece of lead used for ship's ballast
- a block of rock-salt
- a parcel of hemp fibre weighing about two and a half pounds
- a small cushion used in knitting
- one of the smaller moulds used for casting iron
- all of the above

To allay such confusion (hint: "all of the above"), here is a handy guide to clarify.

A **pig** is usually a young animal, weighing less than 120 lbs. A **hog** usually refers to a larger pig (see Porcine Patois, Part Two), and **swine** refers to any of the ungulate mammals of the family *Suidae*.

To be **swinish, hoggish, or piggish** is to be acting like a pig ("greedy and dirty," one misguided reference suggests), especially eating like one.

 To be on the pig's back is to be prosperous.

To go to pigs and whistles means to be ruined. This is thought to perhaps be the origin of many English pubs named "The Pig and Whistle."

A **piggy bank** is a child's bank, in the shape of a pig. Pigs formed of pottery and porcelain are the most popular; a 2,000-year-old Egyptian glazed pottery pig may be one of the very first piggy banks, for it has a slot on its back. But piggy banks were designed to be broken in order to obtain the coins inside, so the original piggy bank or **money pig**, as it is sometimes called, may never be found. The earliest true example in existence traces back only to the end of the eighteenth century, although written references to piggy banks were made in England in the early 1600s. A **pig-penny-horse** is a bank in the form of a horse.

To **drive pigs** is to snore; to **call hogs** is also to snore: "I couldn't sleep a wink with him callin' hogs right next to me."

Pig iron is crude iron, cast in blocks or "**pigs**."

A **pig bed** is a bed of sand in which the pigs of iron are cast.

Piggywhidden is a Cornish word for the smallest or youngest of the litter; a runt.

Pigsney comes from the Middle English *piggesnye* or "pig's eye," originally a term of endearment meaning, literally, "cute little pig's eye." It is thought to have been introduced by Geoffrey Chaucer, who is credited with inspiring the romantic tradition of sending love notes on Saint Valentine's Day in the "Miller's Tale" of his *Canterbury Tales*: "She was a prymerole, a piggesnye, / For any lord to leggen in his bedde, / Or yet for any good yeman to wedde."

In a pig's ear means nonsense. Similarly, **in a pig's eye**, and **in a pig's ass**, but use caution with the latter.

Pig's Eye is also a name for the cuckoo-flower, *Cardamine pratensis*. It was the first name for that vicinity in Minnesota that became the capital city of Saint Paul.

Pig's ear is a Cockney term for beer, and also a flat puff pastry.

A **pigtail** is a plait of braided hair that hangs down one's back. It is also a term for a twisted roll of tobacco.

In a pig's whisper is a reference to time, meaning merely an instant.

The pigs ran through it means "someone upset the apple-cart."

To **hear as a hog in harvest** means "in at one ear and out at the other."

During the Spanish-American War, the United States was referred to as **Yankee Pigs**.

Pigskin is the skin of a pig, another name for a football, or leather made from the hide of a pig. It is also another name for a saddle in Britain, where "To throw a leg across a pigskin," is to mount a horse.

To buy a **pig in a poke** (poke is an old-fashioned name for a small bag) means to buy without looking at what's inside. That way, one may purchase, unseen, a "pig" that might be smaller than anticipated or something that isn't a pig after all. In England's early days, you might get the runt of the litter this way, for peasants often tried to sell small pigs without opening the bag, using the excuse that it would be too much work to catch the piglet if it escaped. This may be the source of the fifteenth century saying, "When a pig is offered, hold open the poke." Occasionally a cat was sold in the unopened bag to the unwary customer. The French version of this, "*acheter chat en poche,*" and the German, "*Man Kauft die Katze nicht in Sack,*" refer to the old trick of selling a cat in a bag and not a suckling pig as advertised. Whoever opened the bag to look inside "let the cat out of the bag."

Thus, **when a pig is offered, hold open the poke,** is advice to seize your opportunities.

To **squeal like a stuck pig** is to squeal loudly with piercing cries.

Someone who is a **pighead** (or **pig-headed**) is an obstinate person, stubborn as a pig.

Pigweed (a.k.a. "Lamb's quarters" or "redroot") is a commonly found, pesky weed.

Like pigs to the slaughter means obediently, disparingly, and in large numbers.

Like stealing acorns from a blind pig is something that's very easily done.

On the other hand, a **blind pig** is also a place where one can purchase illicit liquor.

If you need something **like a pig needs a hip pocket**, you really have no need at all.

Too many pigs for the tits means too many people need something and there's not enough to go around.

A **whistle pig** is another name for a groundhog.

A **piggin** is a small wooden pail or tub with a handle that's formed by continuing one of the staves above the rim.

Pigs in blankets may be oysters or chicken livers wrapped in bacon, skewered and broiled, or they may be hot dogs wrapped in bacon or dough and then cooked.

A **pigstick** is an instrument used for hunting wild boar.

Pig's Nose is a kind of apple.

Pig's Mouth is another name for Toadflax, also known as **Pig's Chops**.

Pig's Foot is another name for birdsfoot-trefoil. This is also known as **Pig's Pettitoes**.

Pettitoes are a term for tiny pig's feet, sometimes used for baby's feet when reciting the following nursery rhyme: *The pettitoes are little feet, / And the little feet not big; / Great feet belong to the grunting hog / And the pettitoes to the little pig.*

Pig's Bubble is another name for cow parsnip (*Heracleum sphondylium*), also known as **Pig's Cole**, **Pig's Flop**.

A **pig-puzzle** is a gate made to swing both ways.

Pig-in-the-Hedge is another name for Blackthorn.

Pig-lily is another name for Arum lily (South African), the root of which is eaten by porcupines, which are sometimes called **Quilly-pigs**.

To **pig it** is "to live in a piglike fashion," says the American Heritage dictionary.

To be as **happy as a pig in mud** is to be content.

If someone is **not fitting to roll with a pig,** it means they're quite uncouth and disgusting.

Long pig was a term was used by Fiji Islanders, in reference to the missionary they had killed, roasted, and eaten. It was not meant to be derogatory; they said "long pig" to differentiate from the other, "short pig," which they enjoyed eating equally well.

To **bleed like a stuck pig** is to bleed freely.

A **pig fish** grunts like a hog and is found in the Atlantic Ocean off the U.S. coast. It is also known as a **hog-fish**.

The **piggery** is the place where pigs are kept.

A sow is **piggy** if she is late in her pregnancy.

A **pig pen** is (a) a pen for pigs; (b) a dirty place (as in, "This room looks like a pigpen!"); (c) a character in the comic strip *Peanuts*, by Charles Schultz.

If someone says, "**If that don't beat a pig a-pecking!**" they mean it's pretty amazing.

A **pig-man** or **pig-wife** is a seller of crockery, in Scotland.

A **pigboat** is slang for submarine.

A **salt pig** refers to the kind of clay originally used to make a small round container that holds salt.

To ride **piggy back** is to ride on the shoulders or back of someone else. This term for carrying one's children on one's back goes back for at least twelve generations. It is also a name for the way in which truck trailers are carried on train cars or specially designed trucks. It is an alteration of the term "pickaback," which may have referred to a pack pitched on one's shoulders for carrying.

To be **pig ignorant** is to be quite stupid (although a pig is actually quite smart).

Pig Latin is a special jargon, sort of like a secret code, in which the initial consonant of each word is transposed to the end of that word with -*ay* added to form a new syllable. The words *Pig Latin* in Pig Latin, would be pronounced *Igpay Atinlay*. In some areas this is called Hog Latin (*Oghay Atinlay*) instead.

A **male chauvenist pig** is a derogatory term that grew out of the Women's Liberation movement in the late 1960s and early 1970s. It refers to a man who is ignorant of or opposes equal rights for women, or maintains a belief in the superiority of his own sex.

(Drawings © Jay Rath)

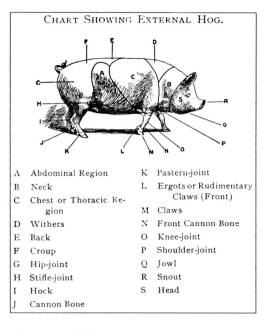

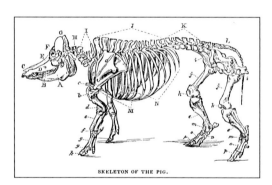

CHART SHOWING EXTERNAL HOG.

A	Abdominal Region	K	Pastern-joint
B	Neck	L	Ergots or Rudimentary Claws (Front)
C	Chest or Thoracic Region	M	Claws
D	Withers	N	Front Cannon Bone
E	Back	O	Knee-joint
F	Croup	P	Shoulder-joint
G	Hip-joint	Q	Jowl
H	Stifle-joint	R	Snout
I	Hock	S	Head
J	Cannon Bone		

The external hog
"Chart Showing the External Hog," from *The Biggle Swine Book* (1906).

The internal hog
"Skeleton of the Hog," from William Youatt's *The Pig* (1847). Authors Charles W. Towne and Edward N. Wentworth (*From Cave to Corn Belt*, 1950), quote paleontologists who conclude that the hog is "the most primitive form of domestic mammal that exists today. From the beginning it has undergone less evolutionary structural change than any other of man's farm and barnyard animals; indeed, less change than man himself."

when the first crop of barley was sown for the year, the farmer's wife would boil a piece of pig meat including the tail, and carry it to the farmer, who would eat some of the pork, then cut off the tail and stick it in the ground to ensure that the ears of barley would grow as long as the tail.

A Hungarian tribe of gypsies known as the Kukuya keeps their hogs from straying by digging a hole in the ground, which they fill with salt and charcoal dust. After replacing the soil they recite:

This is thine,
Come not to us!
I give thee what I can
O Spirit of earth, hear!
Let not the thief go!
We have three chains,
Three very good fairies
Who protect us.

As pigs are quite fond of salt and charcoal, the gypsies know the hogs will root up the hole, but the pigs will not be stolen or run away. To make doubly sure of this, the man in charge of the hogs "runs thrice, while quite naked, round the animal . . . he wishes to protect, and repeats at every turn: *O, thief, do not go, / further do not come! / Thy hands, thy feet / shall decay / If thou takes this animal.*"

A Transylvanian cure for worms in swine is enacted by the hogman who, before sunrise, pours the urine of the hog in question in front of a nettle and chants:

Good, good morrow!
I have much sorrow.
Worms are in my swine today.
And I say, to you I say,

Black are they or white or red
By tomorrow they be dead.

Pig Tales and Traditions Accorded to Other Global Trotters

In Morocco, a wild boar was kept in the stables of wealthy Moors to lure evil spirits from the horses.

The Baluba of the Congo have a woman's association known as the Bulendu. Members may not eat pork because "the spirit of the association" lives in its flesh, yet all women must eat it when they are initiated. However, women of the Lower Congo are not permitted to plant crops if they have eaten pork.

In Celebes, formerly known as Sulawesi, people believe that the spirits of deer and wild hogs can be drawn to a person's home by hanging the jawbones of those animals on the wall. This would imbue the hunter with the animals' spirits as well. In Celebes it is believed that pigs support the earth and are the cause of earthquakes. They also believe that drinking pig's blood induces prophetic powers.

In India pigs are sacrificed to the cholera goddess and disease demons and are thought to propitiate ghosts. And in southern India, as in Celebes, the drinking of pig's blood is felt to inspire powers of prophecy.

The Karens of Burma believe that adultery destroys fertility. When a couple has been found to have committed adultery, the solution is to purchase a hog and kill it. Each partner takes one foot of the pig and makes a furrow. They fill the furrows with blood and pray that having destroyed productivity they may heal it once again.

Marriages among cousins are prohib-

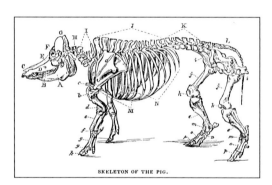

SKELETON OF THE PIG.

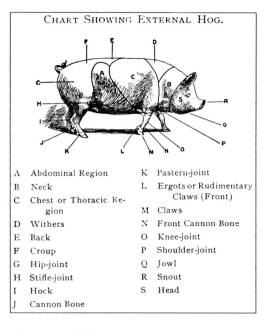

Alone at last
This big sow in Tuscany, Italy, seems almost surprised to find herself without a litter of squealing, hungry piglets. (Photograph © Art Wolfe, Inc.)

Visitors to England are amused and intrigued by charming names given to old inns, such as Boar's Head and Pig & Whistle. There are various explanations for the latter—in Scotland a "pig" is an earthenware pot and "whistle" is small change or petty cash—but a straightforward explanation of a strange phenomenon is likely more accurate. An old English proverb "to go to pigs and whistles" means to be ruined. One wonders which came first, the proverb or the pub?

How to Say "Pig" in Different Languages

Afrikaans: vark
Anglo Saxon: pecga
Arabic: ÎäÒíÑ
Assyrian: Khzooyrraa
Basque: txerri
Bengali: shuor
Breton: moc'h
Bulgarian: svinia
Chinese: zhu
Croatian: svinja
Danish: svin
Dutch: varken
Esperanto: porco
Estonian: siga
Finnish: karkko
French: cochon
Frisian: baarch
German: schwein
Greek: delphax
Hawaiian: pua'a
Hindi: soor
Hungarian: sertés
Icelandic: svín

Indonesian: babi
Italian: porco
Japanese: buta
Latin: porca
Latvian: cuka
Maltese: qazquz
Maori: poaka
Norwegian: gris
Ojibwe: gookoosh
Polish: prosiak
Portuguese: porco
Punjabi: soor
Romanian: porc
Russian: svynya
Sanskrit: varaaha
Slovene: prasa
Spanish: cerdo
Swahili: nguruwe
Tagalog: baboy
Turkish: domuz
Vietnamese: con lo·n
Welsh: mochyn
Yiddish: khazer

Crowded lunch counter

Litters usually consist of eight to twelve piglets, and nursing order is established during the piglet's first forty-eight hours. Once a piglet homes in on a particular teat he will always choose the same one. (Photograph © Jim Steinbacher, courtesy of Leslie Levy Creative Art Licensing, Scottsdale, AZ)

Researchers at Ohio State University have discovered that feeding junk food to pigs makes tastier pork. Studies concluded in 1998 found that pellets made from potato chips destined for the landfill and fed to 250 pigs resulted in juicier, more tender pork chops. Piglets began snacking on the pelleted chips within a week of being weaned.

Tuscan swine
A "drove" is a herd or group of pigs, such as these grazing in Tuscany. (Photograph © Art Wolf, Inc.)

The word "porcelain" is derived from the Italian, *porcella,* meaning "young sow." The French word *porcelaine,* refers to the cowrie-shell, which has the texture of porcelain on one side and resembles the back of a hog on the other.

ited among the Dyaks of Borneo. The prohibition may be lifted by a rather complicated ceremony during which the couple throws their personal ornaments into the water. Then they kill a pig, drain its blood, and throw the carcass into the water, too. Their friends push them into the water and they bathe there together. Finally they fill a joint of bamboo with pig's blood, scattering it as they walk through the neighboring villages.

Zulu girls will not eat pork, for the pig is regarded as an ugly animal, and if they eat its flesh, their children will resemble pigs.

In the Caribbean, it is believed that a girl who eats pork will give birth to children with small eyes.

In China and Japan, a white boar represents the moon and is imbued with the qualities of courage and conquest—characteristics necessary for a warrior. The Chinese have a "pig fairy" known as *Chu Pa-chieh,* which is half-man, half-pig.

Nang-lha is a Tibetan house-god to whom beverages are offered. He is portrayed as a man with the head of a pig.

Lamastu is an Akkadian demoness who causes childhood diseases. The equivalent of the Sumerian Dimme, she is portrayed with bare breasts on which a dog and a pig both feed.

The mythical story of Pele is native to Hawaii. Pele was a young Samoan woman who moved to Hawaii with her family and settled near the crater of the volcano Kilauea in the foothills of Mauna Loa. They seemed unaffected by the volcano, and neighbors thus suspected they possessed supernatural powers. Meanwhile, Kamapuaa, a huge, tattooed beast of a man, lived on the island of Oahu and was referred to as a pig for his evil ways, plundering homes and ravaging young women. He was driven from Oahu and sought out the magical family of Pele, at Kilauea. Pele refused his offer of matrimony and called Kamapuaa a pig. His response was to massacre most of Pele's family. She and a few others hid in a cavern deep inside the mountain. Kamapuaa tried to force his way in when the volcano suddenly erupted. A river of molten rock chased him to the sea, but as a consequence, Pele was forever buried in the mountain. To this day the legend continues that Pele makes the Kilauea shake and the lava flow.

Assorted Auguries and Swine Superstitions

• Pigs that are killed between eight and ten o'clock in the morning will weigh more and be in better condition than they would be if they were killed at a later time of the day.

• In Ireland, it was customary to drive a

pig into the house on the first of May to bring good luck. But a pig that entered a house at any other time during the year was an omen of poverty.

• A popular myth is this: A pig must be slaughtered when the moon is waxing or the meat will shrink in the pot.

• When American novelist John Steinbeck served as a war correspondent for the *New York Herald Tribune* in World War II, he reported that servicemen often carried good luck tokens into battle. One soldier carried a small wooden carving of a pig to which he spoke, saying "Pig, this is not for us," in times of danger.

• One ancient recipe for a healing salve includes stale grease from a boar, powdered bloodstones, powdered worms, and moss from a disinterred human skull.

• To rid yourself of warts, bathe the warts in the blood of a pig (or cat, mole, mouse, or eel).

• Despite the success of Columbus's expeditions, pigs are supposedly unlucky to

Neighbor pig
My learned friend and neighbor Pig,
Odds bobs and bills, and dash my wig!
Tis said that you the weather know;
Please tell me when the wind will blow.
—Mother Goose rhyme
(Photograph © David Lorenz Winston)

HOG.

Pigs can see the wind
Swine weather vane from 1883 mail order catalog, *Copper Weather Vanes, Bannerets and Finials,* manufactured by A. B. & W. T. Westervelt, NY.

have on board a ship. The word "pig" is taboo for a sailor and must not be spoken while at sea for it brings bad luck.

Weather Swine

It has long been claimed that pigs can forecast the weather, and are especially affected by the approach of storms or high winds when they are seen running around their sty with straw in their mouths. In his *Zoonomia, Or the Laws of Organic Life* (1794), Erasmus Darwin made the following observation: "It is a sure sign of a cold wind when pigs collect straw in their mouths, and run about crying loudly. They would carry it to their beds for warmth, and by their calls invite their companions to do the same, and add to the warmth by numerous bedfellows."

• Some farmers believe that pigs can see or smell the wind, meaning pigs are able to detect the approach of a bad storm or a tornado.

• If hogs gaze continually at the sky when nothing is there to draw their attention, a tornado is near.

• When pigs carry straws or twigs in their mouths, it means that rain is coming.

• "When hogs shake the stalks of corn, and thereby spoil them, it indicates rain; and when they run squeaking about and throw up their heads with a peculiar jerk, windy weather is about to commence," says William Youatt in *The Pig* (1847).

• In southeast Missouri during the Civil War, old soldiers claimed that some men used to see the specter of a monstrous black hog just before a battle. This was recognized as a sign that the man who saw the black hog would be killed in action. He told his comrades, made arrangements for letters and keepsakes to

be sent home, and so on. It was said that a man who saw the black boar never lived more than seven days.

Saints and Swine

Saint Anthony was the patron saint of swine and swineherds. "Oh pig . . . so close to the earth, so far from God," he is supposed to have said. In his *History of the Worthies of England* (1662), Thomas Fuller claimed, "St. Anthony is universally known for the patron of hogs, having a pig for a page in all pictures, though for what reason is unknown, except, because being a hermit, and having a cell or hole digged in the earth, and having his general repast on roots, he and hogs did in some sort enter—common both in their diet and in their lodging."

Saint Brannock was told in a dream to build his church where he would find a white sow and her litter. In early Christian legend, the swineherd and his pigs are often involved with the founding of abbeys or churches. In the *Aeneid,* Book VII by Virgil (70–19 B.C.), Aeneas was advised to build his new city in Italy in the place where he would find a white sow with thirty piglets, and thus was the city of Rome founded on the Tiber River. The sow-goddess was named Phaea, or "shining one," so this may be the source of the "white" influence in these stories of both pagan and Christian legend. To the early Celts, the sow was a lunar animal and a symbol of divine inspiration representing death and rebirth. Some Welsh saints built monasteries on sites where they claimed they had been led by a magical white sow.

Saint Leonhard was the patron of cattle, horses, and pigs in Catholic Germany. Models of horses, cows, and pigs

Getting to know you
Child in New York City's "Fresh Air" program gets acquainted with a baby pig. (Photograph © Jerry Irwin)

Mediaeval church carvings of pigs playing bagpipes are plentiful in the United Kingdom, and would have provided models for sign painters illustrating that phenomenon. The term "bagpipes" was sometimes used as a euphemism for a sow's teats.

were dedicated to him, often to ensure the health of the herds and increase their numbers, and sometimes to aid the recovery of sick animals.

A pig's sty is part of the legend of Saint Frideswyde, who took refuge there to escape the unwelcome attentions of Prince Algar. As a young girl she decided to dedicate her life to Jesus Christ, but Frideswyde was very beautiful and many young men were attracted to her beauty and wanted to marry her. Her parents were of no help in fending off these pursuits. When the harassment became too great to endure, Frideswyde packed her things and left home with two companions. They hid themselves in a pig's sty for three years, after which she entered a convent at Oxford.

When Saint Patrick and his followers were dying of hunger, swine came to the rescue. John Gleason, professor of Irish studies at the University of Wisconsin, Milwaukee, says, "According to tradition, St. Patrick once stayed in the home of a nonbeliever during Lent, when the smell of a mutton stew so tempted him to break his meatless fast that he gave in and ate some. Feeling instantly guilty, he repented, and a compassionate angel turned the mutton into salmon, an acceptable Lenten food." But Gleason says the Irish twisted the story a wee bit, and determined that because Saint Patrick was so impressed with the hospitality he was shown, it would be all right for the Irish to eat meat on his feast day. "The meat they ate," Gleason reports, "was the

Guatemalan girl and piglet
Scavenging pigs run freely through this child's rural Central American village. (Photograph © Jerry Irwin)

Saint Anthony, Patron Saint of Swine and Swineherds

The smallest pig of the litter is sometimes referred to as a "Tantony pig," for Saint Anthony, the patron saint of swine and swineherds.

Saint Anthony, also known as Saint Antony the Abbot, was born in Egypt in A. D. 251 to a wealthy family. He was extremely devout from childhood and was considered too sensitive to be sent to school. When his parents died, he placed his sister in a nunnery and gave his considerable inheritance to his neighbors. Then Anthony retired into a state of ascetic solitude, eating only bread with a little salt and spending most of his time in prayer. During this time of self-imposed isolation, which continued for thirty years, he resisted numerous assaults from demonic visitations and hallucinations, many of which appeared in animal form.

Anthony became a model of humility, charity, prayerfulness, and many other virtues. When he finally came down from his mountain near the Red Sea, he founded his first monastery. He died in A.D. 356 on January 17, and this date has become the day on which Saint Anthony is celebrated as the founder of Christian monasticism.

In works of art, Saint Anthony is represented with a crutch, a little bell, a book, and a pig . The pig is present, some sources insist, because of its original association with the devil and the sensual vices with which Anthony was tempted. The pig is also supposed to have been his only companion in his self-imposed solitude—a pleasant but disputable fact.

The pig may have additional significance: When Anthony visited Barcelona, he was sup-posedly asked to heal the son of the King of the Lombards. Before doing so, he heard of a sow in that same town with a lame and blind piglet, which he healed before then healing the prince. Then, in 1096, the Hospital Brothers of St. Anthony were founded. Eventually they established hospitals in Vienna and in other countries. The Brothers of St. Anthony were revered for their charitable work, and they customarily hung a bell around the neck of one of the sows in their herds to let people know they were coming. For their generosity and compassion, the brothers were allowed to feed their swine upon acorns and beech mast and to let them freely scavenge (which was usually forbidden).

Saint Anthony's hospital was founded in London in 1242 by monks of the order of Saint Anthony, who were known for their treatment of Saint Anthony's Fire, a disease caused by eating grains affected with ergot, a fungus parasite. The hospital burned in 1666, but until that time the monks kept pigs for the benefit of their patients, supplying them with meat and lard to treat their diseases of the skin. The pigs were donated to the monks by the general populace—they were usually pigs that were unsellable for one reason or another—and the Proctor of the hospital provided the pigs with bells to wear around their necks, so they would be allowed to run free and scavenge on the streets. The pigs were very tame and would follow anyone who fed them, hence the term "Tantony pig," sometimes used to refer to the runt of the litter or to a person who showed sporadic loyalty.

Saint Anthony of Egypt

Saint Anthony of Egypt treating patient afflicted with St. Anthony's Fire. The Patron Saint of Swine and Swineherds, Anthony has also been appealed to as the patron of domestic animals and farm stock. Guilds tradesmen such as butchers and brush makers have also placed themselves under his protection. He is usually depicted with a crutch, a little bell, a book, and a pig.

Relaxation techniques
A massage can deliver some of us to Hog Heaven any time of the day, just like this little blue-back having its belly rubbed at Marsh Farm, Honeybrook, Pennsylvania. (Photograph © David Lorenz Winston)

French-speaking pirates invented the word "barbecue," referring to a Caribbean pork feast as *de barbe et que*, meaning the pig could be consumed from "beard to tail," or snout to toe. Natives of Hispaniola taught Spanish Buccaneers to cook pig on a frame made of green wood called a *barboca*, inventing the original barbecue.

last of the cured pork set aside from the previous fall's final slaughter."

In some parts of Italy, the common woodlouse is known as *porcello di San Giovanni*, or the piglet of Saint John.

The book *Beasts and Saints*, translated by Helen Waddell (1934) records the story of Saint Malo. As he was walking throughout Brittany to spread the gospel, Saint Malo came upon a grieving swineherd in a meadow. The swineherd had been herding a drove of pigs and one of them, a bold old sow, began to destroy a field of standing corn. In trying to save his neighbor's crop, the swineherd threw a stone at the sow and unintentionally killed her. Now, in addition to his lord's wrath, Saint Malo worried about "the seven piglings trotting about, trying to draw milk as of old from their dead mother's dugs and able to find no stay for their own lives from that lifeless body." Saint Malo was very compassionate and began to cry along with the swineherd. He then touched the ear of the dead sow with his staff and brought her back to life. The swineherd told the story to his master and the master gave one of his farms to the church out of gratitude.

There is a French proverb, *A chaque porc vient Saint Martin*, that means, "Saint Martin comes to every pig." This has been interpreted by a Catholic scholar to mean that Saint Martin helps any person who is humiliated by the circumstances of his or her life, whether it's slavery, poverty, or some injustice that makes that person feel less human, less a member of human society.

An udder source for fast food
Bossy fills a couple orders for a quick drink of milk. (Photograph © J. C. Allen & Son Inc., West Lafayette, IN)

Porcine Patois, Part Two: How to Tell Hog Heaven from Hogwash

A **hog** usually refers to a large pig. It can also be an epithet for someone who is self-indulgent, gluttonous, or vulgar, as in the Hawaiian legend of Pele, who called the beast Kampuaa a "hog."

To be **hog tight** refers to pastures that are fenced with woven wire, to keep the hogs penned in. Perhaps it also means one is reluctant to spend that ten-penny coin.

To **hog tie** something is to tie together its legs to render it helpless.

To **hog down** the corn is to be turned loose in fields to feed on corn or other crops meant for hog consumption.

To be **hog drunk** is an old term meaning the same thing as **swine drunk**, meaning excessively so.

A **road hog** is a driver who "hogs" the road, takes up more space than he is legally allotted; to take more than he is due.

A **hogchoker** is a kind of fish, so poor that it isn't even worth feeding to the hogs.

Hogget is another name for hog, in British dialect.

Hoggin is a natural mixture of gravel and clay, used for constructing roads or paths.

A **hog** is also a kind of broom used for scraping the underwater parts of a vessel, the **hog piece** or **hog stave** portion of the keel. A hog may also refer to a large railway locomotive, or a motorcycle made by Harley Davidson, or it can be a machine used by the lumber industry that grinds slabs of wood into small pieces for fuel.

The **hog score** is a term used in the sport of curling.

Hog fat means fat enough but not *too* fat ("She was not hog fat; she could see her toes.").

To **drive one's hogs to market** is to snore

very loudly. ("He snored so loud we thought he was driving his hoggs to market," said Johnathan Swift in 1738).

Hog's Back is a part of Niagara Falls.

A **hogback** is something thought to resemble the arched back of a hog. In golf, it's a ridge of ground or a hole that has a ridge on the fairway.

Hogg is a term used in Britain for a young sheep before its second shearing.

The **hog-nosed skunk** and **hog-nose snake** have snouts that resemble the pig's.

A **hogshead** is a measure of volume that goes back for over six hundred years and has ranged from 62.5 to 140 gallons. In the United States a hogshead refers to liquid measure, especially the equivalent to 63 wine gallons.

Hogwash is garbage fed to hogs. It also refers to something worthless or false. *The Oxford English Dictionary* of 1440 refers to such swill fed to swine: "They in the kechyn, for iape, pouryd on here hefd hoggyswasch." Translation: "They in the kitchen, for jest, poured hogwash on her head."

To go **hog wild** is to be crazy with excitement, out of control.

To **go whole hog** is to do something to the highest possible degree. There are various theories about the origin of this expression. One says that **to go whole hog** was a sarcastic term that came about in the eighteenth century during the time that the English shilling was known as a "hog." A spendthrift, willing to spend an entire shilling to entertain a friend in a pub, was willing to "go whole hog."

A **hog** was also the name for a ten-penny coin in Ireland, so that **going the whole hog** might be a comment on extravagance, maybe sarcastically so. The expression first appeared in print in the United States in 1828, with the suggestion that one supports wholeheartedly, stops at nothing, goes all the way.

Hog waller refers to a hog wallow, or a piece of land where the ground has small holes that fill with water.

If something is **big enough to choke a hog**, it is probably big enough to choke a cow.

To **hog and panther** someone is to cajole or henpeck them.

Hog age refers to male adolescence, that awkward time between boyhood and manhood.

If someone is **eating high off the hog**, it refers to an expression that came about in the nineteenth century when the British army saw that enlisted men received shoulder and leg cuts of pork while officers were treated to cuts from the top loin.

Hog killing weather refers to cool, autumn weather, the time when hogs were traditionally butchered.

Hog Heaven is, theoretically, the place where the hog's spirit goes after the hog is butchered. But used colloquially, it refers to an idyllic place usually referred to in a light-hearted manner.

A **hogger** is a person who raises hogs. It can also refer to a railroad engineer.

Hog and hominy is another way of referring to pork and cornbread: plain but nourishing rations.

To **hog off the corn** is to turn the hogs out into the cornfield so they will clean up the ears left behind after harvesting.

To say "**that's another hog off the corn**" means there is one less person to feed.

To hog can also refer to planting one's field with grain without plowing the soil first. "He hogged his wheat in this spring." It may also mean to cut timber in a wasteful manner.

A **hoggery** is a British term, like piggery, meaning where hogs/pigs are kept.

A **hogmolly** is the same as a **hogsucker**, of the genus *Hypentelium* and found in clear, cool streams of the eastern United States.

A **hog-leg** is a pistol; "He had a hog-leg in his belt."

To know as much about something **as a hog knows about Sunday** is not to know very much at all.

That's the way the hog bladder bounces means that's the way things go. *C'est la vie.*

To be **as independent as a hog on ice** is not to be very independent, for hogs have a hard time moving about on a slippery surface with their pointed little hooves. In fact, if hogs were to find themselves on ice, their legs might very well slide out from under the poor creatures, or they might very well be spread-eagled, unable to get up again. The saying, however, indicates cocky independence, supreme confidence, and is a very old saying in the United States.

(Drawings © Jay Rath)

Cause for celebration
National Pig Day is celebrated in the United States on March 1. Established in 1972, the day honors pigs as one of the most intelligent and interesting domestic animals. (Photograph © Lynn M. Stone)

Chapter 4

Porcine Pedigrees: From *Porcus* Trojanus to *Porcus* Pygmy

Look at Pork alone. There's a subject! If you want a subject, look at Pork!
—Charles Dickens, *Great Expectations* (1862)

A good fat pig
Facing page: "A good fat pig to last you all the year" was a traditional holiday wish at the turn of the century, along with "A pocketful of money, and a cellar full of beer." Pigs were a favorite subject of greeting card artists. One especially popular card, depicting a herd of rollicking piglets escaping a sty, read, "Excuse haste and a poor pen." (Photograph © Keith Baum/BaumsAway!)

"American Farm-Mortgage Removers"
Inset: From F. D. Coburn's *Swine in America* (1916). It takes only three months, three weeks, and three days to give birth to a litter of piglets. And they can begin to reproduce at the age of one year. Therefore, a single sow could produce seven million offspring in ten generations!

The early Romans had a name for the art of breeding, rearing, and fattening hogs; they called it *Porculatio*, and they tried everything possible to bestow the finest flavor upon their pork. In *The Pig*, William Youatt explained: "The poor animals were fed, and crammed, and tortured to death in various ways, many of them too horrible to be described, in order to gratify the epicurism and gluttony of this people. Pliny informs us that they fed swine on dried figs, and drenched them to repletion with honeyed wine, in order to produce a diseased and monstrous-sized liver. The *porcus Trojanus*, so called in allusion to the Trojan horse, was a very celebrated dish, and one that eventually became so extravagantly expensive that a sumptuary law was passed respecting it. This dish consisted in a whole hog, with the entrails drawn out, and the inside stuffed with thrushes, larks, beccaficoes, oysters, nightingales, and delicacies of every kind, and the whole bathed in wine and rich gravies."

DIAGRAM SHOWING THE DIFFERENT CUTS OF MEAT.

Pork diagram
An illustration from *The Biggle Swine Book* (1906) shows the difference between cuts of meat.

"Now, there is no point of view from which a really corpulent pig is not full of sumptuous and satisfying curves. You can look down on a pig from the top of the most unnaturally lofty dogcart . . . You can examine the pig from the top of an omnibus, from the top of the Monument, from a balloon, or an airship, and as long as he is visible, he will be beautiful. In short, he has that fuller, subtler and more universal kind of shapeliness which the unthinking . . . mistake for a mere absence of shape. For fatness itself is a valuable quality. While it creates admiration in the onlookers, it creates modesty in the possessor."
—G. K. Chesterton, *The Uses of Diversity* (1920)

But such a feast was (thankfully) rare, and more likely the early domesticated pig was raised in a household setting where it became, as mentioned in Robert Malcolmson and Stephanos Mastoris's 1998 book *The English Pig*, "a sort of edible pet." Butchering day was a celebration, and almost no part of the pig went to waste.

"We really meant no harm to the pig. It was just that it happened to be the central figure in the drama," says Thomas Husdon Middleton in *Food Production and the War* (1923). "Much care had been lavished on him, to bring it up to him up to sixteen or eighteen score pounds and now, we thought, he should be almost as proud as we were, that such pleasure for us would ensue from the final act."

Breeding swine with the intention of changing the animal's character and improving its qualities appears to have been a practice that was pioneered in China. From their earliest history, the Chinese have raised pigs in a highly developed, domesticated form, and their stock has contributed greatly toward the improvement of western breeds.

Breeds of hogs were once divided into "bacon" hogs or "lard" hogs. Most early hogs were raised to be quite large and fat. Then in the early 1900s, the frame size of hogs was reduced from the very large lard-type to the smaller, very fat, roly-poly lard-type hogs known as "cob-rollers." In North America during and after World War I, the preference type shifted back to the larger "bacon" strains. These types became known as "meatless wonders," because although they were prolific and lacked excess lard, they were awkward when farrowing and many litters were lost when the sows laid on them.

During the 1930s, meat packers encouraged a move back to the "lard type" hog again, with a focus on the thickness of the fat, as people developed a variety of practical uses for lard. Pie crusts were flaky and tender when lard was used as shortening. Bars of soap were concocted from a combination of lard and lye. Lard was also one of the ingredients used to manufacture nitroglycerine for explosives used during World War II.

With the invention of vegetable oils in the 1960s, and a renewed concern for a healthier diet and leaner meat products, pork producers began to concentrate their efforts toward the production of a leaner hog that would provide meat low in cholesterol and fat. They succeeded: Today's pork is 50 percent leaner than it was only forty years ago.

To the early American farmer, the hog earned its nickname as a "mortgage lifter." A farmer in 1850 might pay five dollars for a sow already bred, and twelve months later he would have her ready to farrow another litter of piglets. At least three or four of her original litter also would be ready to farrow by that time, and the older sow might have another litter in the fall. Even if that farmer only saved and bred two-thirds of his pigs, he'd find his investment appreciating at an amazing rate.

The United States Department of Agriculture (USDA) reported that 105 million hogs were produced in the United States in 1998. Pork production has expanded from the Corn Belt into regions such as Colorado, Arkansas, and North Carolina, where hog-raising practices changed dramatically. Mega-hog operations in these states average 2,400 sows or more. North Carolina now leads the

Spotted Poland China enjoys a cool bath
This monstrous porker weighed 1,000 pounds
and was named "Go Get 'Em." He sired many
Minnesota State Fair blue ribbon champions in
the mid-1950s. (Minnesota State Fair collection)

The heaviest hog ever recorded was a belly-dragging
Poland China named "Big Bill," who weighed 2,552
pounds and measured nine feet long in 1933. He was
owned by Burford Butler of Jackson, Tennessee.

Plump little bodies

Plump little bodies as pink as a rose
Bare as the day they were born, I suppose,
Innocent cupids with neat little toes,
And sly grimace . . .
—French dramatist and poet Edmond Rostand waxes lyrical and romantic when he describes pink newborn piglets in his 1911 poem *Les Cochons Roses*. (Photograph © David Lorenz Winston)

The line-up

Studies have shown that the four front teats give the most milk, and generally these are nursed by the larger and stronger pigs. Thus there *is* some basis for the observation that the runt always "sucks the hind tit." (Photograph © J. C. Allen & Son Inc., West Lafayette, IN)

"Domesticated pigs are marvelously diverse in shape, size, features and colors. The sway-backed, pot-bellied, wrinkle-skinned lard pigs of south east Asia are in sharp contrast to the long, lean white breeds of western Europe; the thick, curly coat of eastern Europe's Mangalitsa defies its relationship with the hairless miniature cuino of Central America. Comparing the squashed face of an English Middle White with the long, tapering snout of an Iberian in Spain or Italy, is like comparing the profile of a Pekingese dog with that of a wolf. Yet nearly all the widely different pigs of Asia and of Europe share the same wild ancestor, a single species within a diverse family of wild pigs."
—Valerie Porter, *Pigs: A Handbook to the Breeds of the World* (1993)

Look-alikes
A dapper gentleman and his pig both smile for the camera in this vintage photograph (circa 1920). (Minnesota Historical Society)

"A Trio of Kansas Reared Berkshires," from F. D. Coburn's *Swine in America* (1916).

The highest known price ever paid for a hog went to Jeffrey Roemisch of Hermleigh, Texas, for a cross-breed barrow named "Bud," who sold for $56,000 on March 5, 1985.

nation in pig production, and the largest sow farm in North Carolina is home to 11,000 sows. These large production facilities are becoming more and more common, producing approximately 40 percent of the nation's slaughter hogs in 1998. They are highly coordinated, capital- and management-intensive operations and have the capability of controlling production to hit specific market targets.

Due to advances in animal genetics, technology, and management practices, more hogs are raised indoors than ever before, and large hog operations are specialized to focus on only one or two particular stages of hog production at different sites. One site might handle only breeding herds, another might handle farrowing activities or nurseries, and yet another might be concerned only with something called "finishing units," where the mature hogs are moved on to markets.

Modern hog breeders have to be ex-acting when meeting the nutrient requirements of their herd, when treating disease, and when using the specialized equipment that turns swine breeding into the very opposite of a "mortgage lifter"—it is a major capital outlay that may require the assumption of a hefty mortgage. The biggest expense in raising hogs is feed. In the first six months of life, the average hog increases in weight by more than 6,000 percent, and avid pork producers want to make their hogs gain this same amount in four or even three months. The second biggest expense is the cost of carrying the brood sow through gestation and nursing; most hog producers want their sows to produce at least two litters of ten offspring per year.

And success isn't automatic. In her 1993 book *Dino, Godzilla and the Pigs: My Life on Our Missouri Hog Farm*, Mary Elizabeth Fricke has this to say about farrowing: "Occasionally sows farrow unexpectedly in the pens out of doors. This can be a disaster as it usually happens when it is

A Taste for Pork

As touted by the American Pork Producers Council, "Pork, the Other White Meat" is white in terms of color and also similar to chicken in being lean and low in fat and calories these days. But even when pork was fatty and cracklings were crisp, the incomparable flavor of roast pork was celebrated by epicures and glorified in prose. In 1821, for example, British essayist Charles Lamb entertained readers of *The London Magazine* with a tongue-in-cheek essay entitled "A Dissertation Upon a Roast Pig":

Away back in Chinese dark ages a man captured alive a boar-shoat, which he exhibited as a curiosity. The flimsy building in which he kept it caught fire and burned with the shoat in it, and after the blaze had died down the showman, seeking to remove the carcase [sic], put a hand to the half-roasted body of the pig, which still was hot, and blistered his fingers. Sticking these into his mouth to relieve the pain, he got, from particles of the pig's skin that adhered to them, his first taste of roast pork, and was so pleased with its flavor that he called his neighbors and had them taste of it also. Soon everybody who could do so, and whenever it could be done, caught a wild shoat, put it in an inflammable booth, to which he set fire, and so had roast pig. Finally it dawned upon some genius among them that all this roundabout, troublesome, and somewhat expensive way of getting toothsome results from the animal could be obviated by killing it and then cooking it in the manner in which other food was cooked; and from that began the domestication of the wild boar and its physical improvement by the Chinese.

Later, in his *Essays of Elia* (1885), Lamb celebrated the succulence of "suckling pigs" in even more grandiloquent and almost orgiastic discourse:

Of all the delicacies of the whole *mundus edibilis* I will maintain this to be the most delicate. I speak not of your grown porkers—things between pig and pork—these hobbydehoys; but a young and tender suckling, under a moon old, guiltless as yet of the sty; with no original speck of the *amor immunditiæ*, the heriditary failing of the first parent, as yet manifest; his voice as yet not broken, but something between a childish treble and a grumble, the mild forerunner or *præludium* of a grunt.

He must be roasted. I am not ignorant that our ancestors ate them seethed or boiled; but what a sacrifice of the exterior tegument!

There is no flavour comparable, I will contend, to that of the crisp, tawny, well watched, not over-roasted *crackling*, as it is well called; the very teeth are invited to their share of the pleasure at this banquet, in overcoming the coy, brittle resistance, with the adhesive oleaginous—Oh, call it not fat!—but an indefinable sweetness growing up to it—the tender blossoming of fat—fat cropped in the bud—taken in the shoot—in the first innocence—the cream and quintnescence of the child-pig's yet pure food; the lean, no lean; but a kind of animal manna, or rather, fat and lean (if it must be so) so blended and running into each other, that both together make but one ambrosian result, or common substance.

Behold him while he is doing! It seemeth rather a refreshing warmth than a scorching heat that he is so passive to. How equally he twirleth round the string. Now he is just done. To see the extreme sensibility of that tender age; he hath wept out his pretty eyes—radiant jellies— shooting stars. See him in the dish, his second cradle; how meek he lieth! Wouldst thou have this innocent grow up to the grossness and indocility which too often accompany maturer swinehood? Ten to one he would have proved a glutton, a sloven, an obstinate, disagreeable animal, wallowing in all filthy conversation—from these sins he is happily snatched away. . . .

A QUICK STIMULANT, BLOOD PURIFIER & PERMANENT TONIC

SOLD ON A SPOT CASH GUARANTEE
TO REFUND YOUR MONEY
IF IT EVER FAILS.

Ask Your Local Dealer

PREVENTS HOG CHOLERA.

Prepared only by
INTERNATIONAL STOCK FOOD CO.
MINNEAPOLIS, MINN., U.S.A.

EVERY 25 LB. PAIL
SAVES $7.00 IN CORN OR OATS
PURIFIES THE BLOOD, AIDS DIGESTION

3 FEEDS FOR ONE CENT

INTERNATIONAL STOCK FOOD

Advertisement, circa early 1900s, for the International Stock Food Co., Minneapolis, Minnesota. (Minnesota Historical Society)

too cold, too hot, or too rainy and the piglets do not survive. The sow makes herself a nest—a hole in the ground she can wallow in comfortably—but if it rains, this hole becomes a mud pond and the piglets drown in it. Of course, no matter where she farrows, a sow may accidentally lie on her offspring, killing them. And some will deliberately kill and eat their own litters. If there are other sows in the pen they may trample and devour the piglets. Or a sow may have a difficult labor as she lies, undetected, hidden by other sows, and in the course of a night or even a few hours die with her unborn piglets. But these mishaps are more likely to occur when the sows are out of doors, unsupervised. So we try to have all our sows deliver in the controlled, stable environment of the farrowing rooms."

Hogs can be bred throughout the year. Gilts are not bred before they reach the age of one year, but they reach puberty at about six months. Commercial breeders allow the boar to run with the sows, but purebred breeders mate their hogs individually with the boar. Artificial insemination is not popular with hog breeders because boar semen is difficult to store properly.

A sow can produce two litters of piglets per year. Litters usually consist of eight to twelve piglets. That means, if pigs ran the farms and were not limited in reproduction, it wouldn't be long before hogs took over the world. Figure it out: If one sow had six piglets twice a year, and the offspring could reproduce at the age of one year (it's possible), that single sow would, in ten generations, produce six and a half million pigs, give or take a few. It's been estimated that one female wild hog could produce seven million offspring during her lifetime!

The sow is in gestation for approximately 112 days (three months, three weeks, three days) and nurses her litter for two months. Sows reach their optimum size litter with their second or third group of piglets.

Baby pigs are born with needle teeth, also called wolf teeth—two large teeth on each side of the upper jaw. These are usually clipped so the sow's udder and other baby pigs are not damaged. Because nursing order will be established during the first forty-eight hours of a piglet's life (once a piglet becomes attached to a particular teat, he or she will always choose the same one), some old-time hog farmers prefer to leave the needle teeth attached to give the piglet an edge in his or her fight for a nipple.

Standard Domestic Breeds

Three hundred different breeds of hogs are recognized world-wide, but many of them are disappearing rapidly. Forty years ago, Europe could boast a total of seventy native pig breeds. Now only twenty-four remain, and several of those are seriously endangered.

In her 1997 book *A Guide to Raising Pigs*, Kelly Klober says:

The three most popular breeds of swine in the United States now are the Duroc, the Hampshire, and the Yorkshire. They and their crosses are the backbone of the pork industry. Their development and preservation was the loving work of generations of small and mid-size family farmers.

A distinction of sorts is now made between colored and white breeds of swine. Although all of today's swine

breeds are selectively bred for leanness, efficiency and meatier carcasses, the colored breeds are still considered to have better 'economic' traits. As a group they are noted for their vigor, faster yet leaner growth, and meatier carcasses.

The white breeds, on the other hand, are strong in the traits needed for successful pig raising. They milk better than colored breeds and as a group, tend to farrow large litters. They also have the docile nature you need when you are raising and weaning large litters. On commercial farms the goal is to blend these genetics—and thus these breed-specific traits—to produce goodly numbers of hogs that possess the best qualities of the different breeds.

"It's the *Snout*, Stupid!"
It's a fact that pigs have two hearts: one that beats inside their chest and another worn at the end of their noses. The snout of a pig is actually an upside down heart-shape. Strong and flexible, the snout offers the hog an unusual tool—a spade, with which it can root for food. (Photograph © David Lorenz Winston)

Porcine Patois, Part Three:
Knowing Your Pork Can Save Your Bacon

Pork can refer to the flesh of a pig or hog used as food. It can also be used to describe government funds or appointments acquired by a representative for his or her constituency as political patronage.

To **choke on one's bacon** is said of someone so eager to prove himself that he takes unnecessary risks. Example: "He introduced himself and nearly choked on his bacon." or "Don't choke on your bacon," meaning slow down, don't go overboard. This term grew out of the experience of Philip II of Spain, who, during the sixteenth-century Spanish Inquisition, was so determined to prove that he was not a secret adherent of Judaism that he consumed copious quantities of bacon and nearly died.

Pork barrel is slang for a government project or appropriation that will benefit a specific legislator's constituents. Prior to the Civil War in the United States, it was a common practice to distribute salt pork to one's slaves from huge barrels; the term **pork barrel politics** came about after the war, in the 1870s, when congressmen were accused of dipping into the "pork barrel" to obtain funds for popular projects in their home districts. Today terms such as **congressional pork** are still used for similar purposes.

A **porker** is a fattened young pig.

A **pork pie** is a thick-crusted pie filled with chopped pork.

Pork rinds are a form of junk food much favored by cartoon character Homer Simpson and former President George Bush.

A **pork pie hat** refers to a man's hat that has a low, flat crown and a snap brim.

A **slice off the same bacon** is a person or thing that is very similar to another.

Language that would fry bacon refers to profanity or swear words.

To be **hamfisted** is to be clumsily brutal.

Ham radio operators were novices, originally, and somewhat like ham actors (below).

Cracklings are crispy bits of fibrous tissue left in lard after it has been rendered, or the crisp, browned rind of roasted pork.

Chitterlings are the small intestines of ....a pig.

A **ham actor** is definitely not first-rate, probably an abbreviated form of **hamfatter,**

which was a term given to an actor of low grade around 1875. The term is derived from the use of ham fat, which actors used instead of cold cream to remove their makeup.

Souse is a kind of gelatinous meat, like head cheese. Both are made with the meat from the pig's head.

(Drawings © Jay Rath)

Swine basket
A peck of portly piglets. (Photograph © Lynn M. Stone)

Weighing in

Most hogs were once raised in the Corn Belt, an area consisting of twelve Midwestern states: Illinois, Indiana, Missouri, Minnesota, Nebraska, Ohio, Michigan, Wisconsin, Kansas, North and South Dakota, and Iowa. In those days, pork producers managed farrow-to-finish farms, where hogs were bred, born, and raised to market in one location. (Photograph © J. C. Allen & Son Inc., West Lafayette, IN)

Domesticated hogs around the world differ remarkably with regard to shape, color, size, and even coat—some have fur instead of bristles! But a few major breeds are worth noting for their contributions to the healthy crossbreeds that have become plentiful in North America.

The Duroc

This American breed was derived from a cross between the Jersey Red of New Jersey and the Duroc from New York. It was improved after the Civil War, a time when it was known as the Duroc-Jersey. The breed finally received acclaim after the 1893 Columbian Exposition in Chicago, where nine Duroc herds were exhibited. By the turn of the century, red hogs were common in the Corn Belt. They were considered real competition to the Poland China, the most important breed in the area at that time.

The Duroc is reddish in color, with small, drooping ears, and is adaptable to a variety of conditions. There is some dispute as to the origin of the red hogs involved with the foundation of this breed. Some scholars believe reddish brown hogs were prevalent on the Guinea coast of Africa and accompanied slave-trading ships to the United States. Other scholars claim that the hogs brought here by Columbus were red, as were those imported by De Soto in 1539. Early American notables Henry Clay and Daniel Webster imported red hogs from Spain and Portugal for their farms in the early part of the nineteenth century.

The Hampshire

All breeds with "shire" as a suffix are of British origin. The Hampshire we know in the United States is similar to the Essex

Nose Rings and Ear Notches

Hogs root; it's the nature of the beast. The practice of placing rings in a hog's nostrils was developed to prevent them from tearing up pastures and rooting where they're not welcome.

The practice of notching a pig's ear for identification has been in practice for some time. Many farmers prefer ear tags. Others use both notches and tags. The notching system is complex. If you're a piglet, the notches in your right ear (your "litter ear") indicate the litter you were part of. All your siblings have that same notch; it's like your surname. Your left ear, then, is like your first name; it is unique to you, because it appears in a particular quadrant. When combined with your litter-ear notch, your ears will be unlike any other pig's ears on the farm. You can have a minimum of one notch on each ear or a maximum of nine notches on an ear. (I warned you it was complex!) (Photograph © J. C. Allen & Son Inc., West Lafayette, IN)

As I looked out on Saturday last,
A fat little pig went hurrying past.
Over his shoulders he wore a shawl,
Although he didn't seem cold at all.
I waved at him, but he didn't see,
For he never so much as looked at me.

Once again, when the moon was high,
I saw the little pig hurrying by;
Back he came at a terrible pace,
The moonlight shone on his
    little pink face,
And he smiled with a face that was
    quite content.
But never I knew where that
    little pig went.
    —**Traditional**

Tender touch
A farmer revives a chilled piglet, drying it off after farrowing. (Photograph © J. C. Allen & Son Inc., West Lafayette, IN)

Getting a Handle on the Hog

Swineophile or not, terminology is important. If you can't get a grip on hog lingo, Pig Latin might as well be Greek.

Pig: To be absolutely correct, this is a term for a very young pig, but it is used conversationally and informally for animals that have a snout and a short, curly tail, and say "oink."

Piglet or Suckling Pig: An infant hog, from birth to around eight weeks, at which time he or she is weaned and weighs close to thirty pounds.

Hog: If you're a professional hog raiser, this term indicates a swine that weighs more than 120 pounds.

Swine: Same thing as a hog, just sounds more sophisticated.

Gilt: A female less than eighteen months of age that has not yet given birth and is probably still a virgin; akin to a heifer in bovine terms.

Sow: A female hog, and if she's "**piggy,**" she's late in her pregnancy. A sow can be bred at eight months to farrow at the age of one year. A sow is usually more agreeable than a boar unless she imagines a threat to her piglets, at which time she can display extreme aggressiveness. Most sows are bred on a small farm for three or four years, less than that in large commercial pork operations.

Shoat: A recently weaned pig, also known as a "**weaner,**" (but not yet a "wiener"); a pre-adolescent.

Young pig or **Runner**: Larger than a shoat, but not yet a regular hog.

Barrow: A castrated male who usually suffers that indignity before he reaches the age of one week.

Boar: A male pig with all his sexual organs intact. A **he-boar** is a country term for a good-breeding hog. Boars can be proud and aloof unless they become impotent, when they show symptoms of anxiety. A boar is of use on a small farm until he reaches thirty to thirty-six months of age. By then he frequently weighs more than 500 pounds and his daughters are coming into the herd. *Boar* can also refer to the wild boar of the sub-family, *Sus*.

Rig: A male pig with one testicle that has not descended. This may be overlooked at the time of castration, so the hog becomes a frustrated boar.

Stag: An older male pig ready for slaughter.

Farrow: To give birth to one's litter.

Butcher hog: A hog that weighs 220 to 260 pounds and is ready to sell for slaughter (five to seven months of age); may also be known as a **market hog**.

Feederpig: A small pig between eight and twelve weeks old and forty to seventy pounds, sold to a farmer/feeder to be brought up to market weight.

Governments: An old-fashioned term for hogs rejected by the government as unsound. *Swine in America* (1910) said these pigs, ". . . if found to be affected so as to make their flesh unfit for human food, are condemned, slaughtered, and tanked. The tank is a large, steam-tight receptacle, like a steam boiler, in which the lard is rendered under steam pressure. This high degree of heat destroys all disease germs with which the diseased carcass may have been affected. The product of the tank is converted into grease and fertilizer."

Descriptive Terms

Cob rollers: A term coined early in the 1900s, meaning a short, roly-poly, thickly built hog.

Race horses: Taller and flatter-muscled hogs.

Blown apart: A hog with good internal body dimension throughout.

Feed efficiency: How much feed it takes for growth to take place.

Daylight: If a pig has this, he or she has nice long legs because you can see daylight underneath.

Coon-footed: A coon-footed hog has a flatter, more flexible foot that will tolerate concrete or hard surfaces.

Pig parlor: A large, aluminum-roofed barn divided into small stalls with sloping concrete floors, where sows are farrowed, piglets are kept in a nursery, and feeder pigs are raised in "finishing pens"—everything under one roof.

Herd: The size of a herd of swine is usually referred to by the number of breeding sows.

It was not unusual for farmers in America's heartland to feed their hogs on, among other things, undigested corn found in the droppings of cattle. In the early 1930s, the Iowa Agricultural Experimental Station traced the progress of an average pig that followed behind two steers for 120 days and determined the pig had rooted up the equivalent of 312 pounds of corn!

The Duroc
The Duroc breed was named for a horse, a thoroughbred stallion owned by Harry Kelsey of Florida, Montgomery County, New York. Issac Frink, a neighbor of Mr. Kelsey, came over one day in 1823 to take a look at the stallion. While he was at the farm a herd of red hogs caught his eye. He purchased the hogs and since they had no breed name, he called them Durocs, after the stallion. (Photograph © Lynn M. Stone)

and Western Saddleback found in England. The breed is black with a white belt around its shoulders, front legs, and feet. In the mid-1800s there was a fad for breeding cattle and hogs for this belted effect, and P. T. Barnum imported a Dutch Belted cow for his sideshow in 1840, which helped fuel the fire. Today, hogs without a white belt encircling the entire body will not be issued a Hampshire pedigree document, and breeders are left to sell off marked gilts to hog producers who do not discriminate for color. Even when both parents have distinctive markings, it is common for litters to vary in uniformity.

The Hampshire has erect ears and a trim appearance, and the breed was originally known for its hardiness, vigor, and foraging ability. It is one of the original breeds in the United States and, according to the Hampshire Breed Registry, "probably originated from the Old English Breed, a black hog with a white belt that was popular in Scotland." Hampshires were brought to the United States in the 1800s from Hampshire in England and developed in Kentucky. The first registry association for Hampshires was known as the "Thin Rind Record Association."

The Poland China

Among the largest of the modern breeds of swine, the Poland China has a black body with six white points (on its four feet, the tip of its nose, and the tip of its tail). The city of Cincinnati contributed to the popularity of the Poland China breed, a composite of the Big China, Russian, Byfield, Berkshire, and Irish Grazier breeds grown in the counties surrounding that city. In 1833, Cincinnati

The Poland China
Above: Referred to by hog breeders as "Polands," the name is actually a combination of the "Poland and China." The breed was developed in Ohio with a background that included the Irish Grazier, the Spotted China, and the Warren County Hog. The "Poland" element referred to an early Polish immigrant who contributed the progeny of some of his hogs to the improvement of the breed. His name was difficult to pronounce, so his pigs were naturally called "Polands." (Photograph © J. C. Allen & Son Inc., West Lafayette, IN)

Hampshire sow and piglets
Left: This black-and-white belted pig was found in the county of Hampshire, England, where it was also known as the Wessex Saddleback. Other names given to this breed were the Mackay, Ring Middle, Ring Necked, Thin-Rind, and the Rhinoceros Hog. They were not officially christened "Hampshire" until 1904. (Photograph © J. C. Allen & Son Inc., West Lafayette, IN)

Herd of Spotteds
Originally known as Spotted Poland China, this breed descended from a big Poland China sow in Indiana that accidentally had a few spots. Eventually a couple of Gloucester Old Spots were imported from England to improve the breed and create new bloodlines. The Spotted breed became a true farmer's hog, meant to improve local stock and provide good, practical swine. (Photograph © J. C. Allen & Son Inc., West Lafayette, IN)

In terms of pig population, the leading hog producing countries at the present time are: People's Republic of China, United States, Brazil, Germany, Russian Federation, Spain, Poland, France, Netherlands, Canada, Ukraine, Denmark, Taiwan, Mexico, Japan, and the Philippines.

slaughtered or packed 85,000 hogs and was christened "Porkopolis." In 1853, that number grew to 360,000 hogs, and in 1863, during the Civil War, 608,457 hogs were slaughtered and processed there, shipped out of the city by means of the Ohio River. Most of these hogs were Poland Chinas from the surrounding region.

The Spotted

Formerly known as the Spotted Poland China, the Spotted has black and white spots and drooping ears. It produces large litters. These hogs are related to the Gloucester Old Spot, a very old British breed that is now somewhat rare but enjoys support from the Royal Family. The Gloucester Old Spot was known as "the orchard hog."

In the United States, the Spotted breed was developed mainly in Indiana. The Gloucester Old Spot breed was brought in to mix with the Spotted Poland China when two hogs known as King of England 429 and Queen of England 1551 were imported into Indiana in 1914 from the south of England. Today the Spotted Poland China is found throughout the United States and is 50 percent white and 50 percent black with large, even, well-defined spots.

The Berkshire

Officially established in England prior to 1860, the Berkshire was introduced to the United States in 1823. At that time they were unfairly judged as being of inferior size. To counteract this misconception, A. B. Allen of Buffalo, New York, imported a boar named Windsor Castle in 1841. The boar had been bred by the

The Berkshire
Once the most popular pig in England, this breed was typical of the very large, eighteenth-century bacon type. Exports provided a lasting effect on many foreign breeds. (Photograph © Russell A. Graves)

Truffle Hunting

How is it that pigs snuffle for truffles? The definitive text, *Pigs: From Cave to Corn Belt*, carries this explanation from a French *abbé*:

> At the age of six to eight months, pigs are most adapted to doing this work, which consists of indicating the place where the truffles are found by digging into the ground to uncover them. . . . All pigs being fond of truffles, it is only necessary to let a pig taste a truffle, after which it works instinctively, turning the earth to uncover more. With a cord encircling its neck, the animal is closely watched by the operator as it turns up the ground. When the truffles appear, the owner gathers them quickly, lest they be devoured. Sometimes with very greedy pigs, the operator is obliged to turn the earth himself at the place indicated by the pig. To do this, he pulls strongly on the cord to hold the animal back from the place indicated, and with a wooden stick he searches the ground carefully. In order to quiet the hog, the operator gives the animal some kernels of corn or other dainties.

The pig's desire for truffles is not only instinctual, but also consuming, as the following excerpt from Peter Mayle's *Toujours Provence* (1991) illustrates:

> The old man and the pig wandered off into the trees as though they were taking an aimless stroll, two rotund figures dappled by the winter sunshine. . . . A muddy snout the size of a drainpipe poked into the shot, and the pig got down to work, its snout moving rhythmically back and forth, ears flopping over its eyes, a single-minded earth-moving machine.
>
> The pig's head jerked, and the camera drew back to show the old man pulling on the rope. The pig was reluctant to leave what was obviously a highly desirable smell.
>
> "The scent of truffles to a pig," said Alain, "is sexual. That is why one sometimes has difficulty persuading him to move."
>
> The old man was having no luck with the rope. He bent down and put his shoulder against the pig's flank, and the two of them heaved against each other until the pig grudgingly gave way. The old man reached into his pocket and palmed something into the pig's mouth. Surely he wasn't feeding it truffles at 50 francs a bite?
>
> "Acorns," said Alain.

The Yorkshire

He may look like a cross little pig, but this Yorkshire piglet is also known as the Large White and can gain as many as three pounds per day! The breed has spread worldwide and greatly influenced the global pig industry as the basis of commercial crossbred sows. (Photograph © David Lorenz Winston)

Crown of England and at the age of two years tipped the scales at 800 pounds.

The Berkshire breed proved popular in the United States during the 1930s and still enjoys popularity. It is a black breed of hog, with white points and white splashes found in the face and lower half of the body. The Berkshire snout, once short and upturned, was selectively bred out of the species, as it was thought to contribute to food waste and respiratory problems. Berkshire pork is lean and especially revered in Japan where it commands premium prices. (The Black Poland is similar to the Berkshire in color, but it has drooping ears.)

The Yorkshire

Originating in England and similar to the English Large White, the Yorkshire in that country are known as the Large, the Middle, and the Small. It has been the

The Landrace
The background of this popular lop-eared breed goes back to medieval Denmark. One physical peculiarity of the Landrace is the fact that it has sixteen or seventeen pairs of ribs, compared to the usual fourteen. (Photograph © David Lorenz Winston)

97

Champion Chester White, 1930
Although the Chester White is definitely a white hog, hog farmers commonly refer to them as "Chesters." (Photograph © J. C. Allen & Son Inc., West Lafayette, IN)

A fifty-pound sow jumped from a sinking ship when the atomic bomb was tested on Bikini in the mid-1950s, and swam through radioactive waters until she was rescued. Although sterile, "Pig 311," as she came to be known, grew to adulthood and reached a total weight of 500 pounds, living out her days at the National Zoological Park in Washington D.C.

leading breed in Canada for some time and is now the most common breed of swine in the United States as well, although the Large type of Yorkshire is the only one to have gained acceptance here. It was one of the largest breeds when it was introduced to the United States in 1893. Today's Yorkshires may weigh well over 1,000 pounds and can grow at an astonishing rate of more than three pounds per day.

The Yorkshire is an example of one of the "white" breeds of hogs and, as such, is subject to sunburn (although "white" is not really white, but actually a very light shade of tan and a dominant color in swine). In this country, white breeds such as the Yorkshire are referred to as a "Mother Breed," for they have large litters and good milking ability, allowing the sows to raise large litters.

The Landrace
This is the longest of today's popular breeds of swine. It is white, with long, drooping ears, and produces very large litters.

The breed originated in Denmark, with the unusual result that Denmark became known for the bacon it exported to England. In 1934 the U.S. Department of Agriculture imported some Landrace hogs from Denmark and many of these were crossbred to become ancestors of a number of new breeds in this country.

The Landrace is found in many other countries, where it is known as the Italian Landrace, Belgian Landrace, Dutch

Tamworth boar

A nineteenth-century English breeder describes the Tamworth as "a large, coarse, leggy pig, with a straight and thinly-set coat, and a dark chestnut-coloured skin . . . a long, tapering wedge-shaped face and a tail that never curled." He also complained that it could jump over or through or dig under any fence ever invented and was "too prolific by half." (Photograph © J. C. Allen & Son Inc., West Lafayette, IN)

You can adopt a rare Gloucestershire Old Spot pig through the Kelmscott Rare Breeds Foundation. In Britain, farmers used to feed this breed on orchard fruit, resulting in their nickname, "orchard pigs." Adoption fees help support this breed and other endangered livestock kept by the Kelmscott Community, an educational foundation in Lincolnville, Maine.

Landrace, French Landrace, German Landrace, Norwegian Landrace, and Swedish Landrace—all white swine with similar physical characteristics to the original Danish strain where it has always been the dominant breed.

The Chester White

This breed was developed in the United States and was originally known as the Chester County White for its beginnings in Chester County, Pennsylvania. The 1908 publication *Cyclopedia of American Agriculture* commented on the first improvement in the breed: "About the year 1818, Captain James Jeffries imported from England a pair of white pigs, which are spoken of as Bedfordshire pigs and as Cumberland pigs. Captain Jeffries used the boar on the native white pigs of the district with good results. Later, it is stated, white Chinese pigs were imported to Chester County and crossed on the native pigs. Eventually the different strains were combined and from this combination came the original Chester-White breed."

The Tamworth

According to the Tamworth Swine Association, "The Tamworth originated in Ireland where they were called 'The Irish Grazer.' About the year 1812 it is said that Sir Robert Peel, being impressed with the characteristics of them, imported some of them and started to breed them on his estate in Tamworth, England. They have been bred quite extensively ever since they were imported into that country."

This is a light red breed with erect ears and an unfair reputation for bad temperament. The Tamworth snout is moderately long and quite straight. The hog has characteristics of what once used to be called the "range hog" and may be the most vigorous of the swine breeds. Tamworth sows are considered the best mothers of all the colored breeds of swine. Once the Tamworth was used as an example of the ideal "bacon breed."

Some Less Common Breeds

Found primarily in Canada, the **Wessex** (sometimes referred to as the Wessex Saddleback) has the confirmation of the Landrace, including the drooping ears, but the black and white color pattern of the Hampshire.

The fifth most popular breed in Canada, the **Lacombe**, is named after the Alberta town where it was developed. Selective breeding has given this breed its large, drooping ears, short legs, and white color. Lacombes are known for their docility, fertility, and rapid growth rate.

Another breed found mostly in Canada these days, although it is rare in that country, is the **Large Black** of English origin. It is all black with erect ears and possesses innate vigor.

The **Mulefoot** is an endangered species. This hog breed is black, with drooping ears and a solid foot like a mule (not a cloven foot with two toe points, as seen in other swine breeds). The Mulefoot has been given attention by the American Livestock Breeds Conservancy and some affiliated breeders to help provide protection for the breed and to provide alternate genetics for the swine industry. A swine text from the nineteenth century already considered the Mulefoot an old breed of swine at that time. One of the last remaining herds of Mulefoot swine survived only because it was isolated on an island in the Mississippi River where

Potbellied pig

Officially known as "Ì" (surely the shortest breed name in the world), this dwarf swine, developed in the 1960s, was originally imported by Canadian Keith Connell, whose intended to provide the pig to laboratories and zoos. But a frenzy developed when a private buyer purchased one as a pet, and by 1986 the market price ran into the thousands of dollars. (Photograph © Keith Baum/BaumsAway!)

In October 1998, the *Pittsburgh Post-Gazette* reported that Lulu, a pet potbellied pig, saved the life of her owner, Jo Ann Altsman, after the woman had collapsed from a heart attack. Knowing something was wrong, Lulu went outside, past the yard, where she had never gone before. Witnesses saw Lulu wait until a car approached, then walk onto the road and lay in front of the vehicle. The driver stopped for the prone pig and got out of his car. Lulu then led the man to the house where Altsman lay. An emergency crew arrived on the scene shortly after he called for help.

Pigs as Pets

The popularity of keeping a pig around the house is not a strange new fad. In fact, sad to say, it's a craze that may have already come and gone. Potbellied pigs were first imported into the United States in 1985, and prices skyrocketed, but owners soon discovered their pet porkers could tip the scales at more than 300 pounds without a whole lot of encouragement. Animal rescue groups such as Pigs Without Partners of Los Angeles, or L'il Orphan Hammies in Solvang, California, provide homes for pigs that have "overgrown" their welcome.

If a potbellied pig owner watches the pig's diet, the pig may top out at only 100 to 150 pounds. Pig breeders are attempting to breed a smaller, "micro pig" more suitable for apartment living.

Pigs are popular pets because hogs can be housebroken. And, like a dog, they can learn to attract their owner's attention when they have to go outside. Pigs openly express their fondness for certain humans—they have been observed greeting a favorite visitor with affection and even joy, inviting caresses and a scratch on the back.

"Miss Pig"
Long before the potbellied pig phenomena, writer G. K. Chesterton expressed his boyhood dream to have a pig as a pet in *The Uses of Diversity* (1920): "I could never imagine why pigs should not be kept as pets. To begin with, pigs are very beautiful animals. Those who think otherwise are those who do not look at anything with their own eyes, but only through other people's eyeglasses." (Photograph © Leslie M. Newman)

Potbellied piglet
What could be more fun than playing with a potbellied piglet? Fanciers found they may be small and cuddly when young, but the average weight of a potbellied pig is close to 100 pounds, and some are not especially fond of being picked up or held. (Photograph © David Lorenz Winston)

If you live where cold or damp weather is frequent, you should purchase colored pigs, as they will be hardier due to their colored-breed parents. White pigs are appropriate for hot weather, because they are more tolerant to heat.

The Minzhu

China has long been recognized as the world's largest pig producer. The USDA estimated that in 1997 the People's Republic of China produced close to 500 million pigs. This pig, a Chinese Minzhu breed, has the big ears, dipped back, and drooping belly typical of most Chinese swine breeds. (Photograph © Joseph Stanski)

The Hereford
The Hereford is a red and white hog, with a pattern similar to that in the Hereford breed of cattle. It has a white face, red body, and drooping ears. This is a relatively new breed, with foundation stock chosen as recently as 1934. (Photograph © Lynn M. Stone)

"The Hog's Breath Saloon," famous for its Key West, Florida, location, originated in Fort Walton Beach, Florida, in 1976. The name came from a phrase used by the grandmother of the owner, Jerry Dorminy, who used to say, "Bad breath is better than no breath at all," and the bar's well-known logo (found on Hog's Breath T-shirts) features a colorful wild boar.

it lived on its own; its survival is a testament to the hardiness of the breed.

Pigs of the Wild

We've already devoted an entire chapter to "The Wild Boar in the Wood," *Sus scrofa*, so it seems only fair to review a few other familiar wild pigs in passing.

The **wart hog** is as ugly as one might expect. About thirty inches tall at the shoulder, this relative of our domestic pig is a drab, dark brown color with a large, homely head totally out of proportion to its body. The wart hog is disfigured by facial warts and protuberances, including the largest tusks in the entire hog family. There's also a tuft of hair at the end of its fifteen-inch tail and long stiff bristles at the top of its head and neck.

The **giant forest hog** is found in Africa. It's the largest of all the wild pigs, weighing in at a gigantic 600 pounds or more. It has a brown bristly coat, facial warts, and despite its imposing appearance is, according to scientists, rather shy.

Razorbacks is a name for the feral pigs of Arkansas, where they have been found roaming around since some of de Soto's swine ran off in the 1540s. Today's razorbacks barely resemble the original razor-backed hogs (so-named for the razor sharp tusks of the boars) who were said to be as "fast as horses, shifty as jackrabbits and, when cornered, ferocious as tigers."

The **babirusa** is a peculiar beast no matter how you look at it—there's an extra sac found in its stomach to aid digestion of cellulose; it likes to live near water, preferring marshes, swamps, and dense jungle; it is a good swimmer and a fast runner. But the strange tusks of the male that have fascinated animal scientists: They have two sets of apparently useless tusks, developments of the canine teeth. The lower canines curve upward and backward toward the skull, but in a smaller semi-circle and closer to the snout than the upper canines. The upper canines are directed upward from the jaw and, after piercing the snout, they curve backward in a semi-circle that, eventually, if they are not worn down or lost in combat, will pierce the Babirusa's skull and kill it.

Other interesting wild pigs are the **riverhog** or **bushpig**, common in Africa and Madagascar; only the males of this species have warts. Males of the **bearded pig** have warts but these warts are somewhat disguised due to the general hairiness of the face, including, as one writer put it, "bushy white cheek tufts that give the species its name but are more like an overgrown moustache and sideburns than a beard."

Then there's the tiny **pygmy hog** of the Himalayan foothills, which has the distinction of being one of the most endangered species of mammals, for there are only about 100 pygmy hogs remaining in the world. It weighs between thirteen and twenty-two pounds, is about twenty-three inches long with a wee one-inch tail. There are no warts on this cute little creature. It has a band of short, dark hair beneath each eye and a brown, furry coat. The pygmy hog can be tamed, but it is nervous and shy.

"Jerry's Old Town Inn," in Germantown, Wisconsin, is famous for its barbecued ribs and pig decor. In 1998 the restaurant sold forty tons of ribs; Jerry's is among the top three restaurants in the United States in pork usage per restaurant operation, but it's number one in the nation when it comes to pork usage per restaurant seat.

Wild pigs are causing problems in parts of Costa Rica and areas of the United States where feral hogs have reverted to characteristics of their wild ancestors. An estimated one million wild pigs (who arrived 450 years ago with Spanish conquistadors and never left) are rooting up Florida farm fields, hogging food from endangered animals and even trotting across the shuttle runway at Kennedy Space Center, where a special team stands ready to frighten them away.

Peccaries

A distant relative of the pig (sort of like a second cousin once removed), the javelina or peccary originated in South America. While it has some similarities to our domestic hog (the same kind of snout and feet), the head is more like that of the wild boar. Peccaries are found in the southwestern United States and in Latin America. (Photograph © Michael H. Francis)

Wart hog

Above: A native of Africa and named for its unfortunate facial warts, this is not a very pretty pig. It lives entirely on grassy plants and scoops out grass roots during the dry season with the tough upper edge of its nose. (Photograph © Art Wolfe, Inc.)

Barbirusa

Left: A true pig, even though its name taken from the Malay words *babi* (hog) and *rusa* (deer) means, literally, "hog-deer." The French version of its name (*cochon-cerf* or "pig-stag") also refers to the dramatic tusks found on this uncommon animal. (Photograph © Art Wolfe, Inc.)

Chapter 5

A Pig Is a Pal Who'll Boost Your Morale

All animals are equal. But some animals are more equal than others.
—George Orwell, *Animal Farm* (1945)

Piglet

Facing page: There are many famous pig characters in entertainment, but arguably the most famous piglet is Winnie the Pooh's gentle, modest best friend, aptly named Piglet. Like Pooh Bear, Piglet was the original creation of A. A. Milne, author of *Winnie the Pooh* (1926) and *A House at Pooh Corner* (1928). And, like Pooh, Piglet was a character based on one of Milne's son Christopher Robin's stuffed nursery toys. British artist E. H. Shepherd drew the original version of Piglet for Milne's books. The "modern" version of Piglet, seen here, first appeared on the big screen in *Winnie the Pooh and the Blustery Day* (Walt Disney Pictures, 1968). (© Disney Enterprises, Inc.)

Oinkabet

Inset: "A-B-C," from the cross-stitch pattern "Oinkabet," designed by Barbara Christopher for Jeanette Crews Designs and cross-stitched by Kathryn A. Coyle, DVM. (© Jeanette Crews Designs, Inc.)

Pigs in Literature

Toward the end of Thomas Pynchon's 1973 novel *Gravity's Rainbow*, Slothrop and the pig are wandering across the countryside together. The pig seems to know where she's going:

A pig is a jolly companion,
Boar, sow, barrow, or gilt—
A pig is a pal, who'll boost your
 morale,
Though mountains may topple
 and tilt.
When they've blackballed, bam-
 boozled, and burned you,
When they've turned on you, Tory and Whig,
Though you may be thrown over by Tabby or Rover,
You'll never go wrong with a pig, a pig,
You'll never go wrong with a pig!

Indeed, authors and poets seem to agree "you'll never go wrong with a pig," for hog heroes and heroines add their own personality to novels and poems written as far away as yesteryear and as long ago as yesterday, enhancing the inherent traits of swine in a variety of luminous (if not always radiant) ways.

Woodcut, from an eighteenth-century children's book
In his *History of Four-Footed Beasts* (1658), Edward Topsell writes of the hog, "It seemeth a special work of God which hath made this tame beast so fruitful, for the better recompense to man for her meat and custody."

In his *Through the Looking Glass and What Alice Found There*, Lewis Carroll wrote a poem entitled *Jabberwocky*, which began:

> 'Twas brillig, and the slithy toves
> Did gyre and gimble in the wabe;
> All mimsy were the borogroves,
> And the mome raths outgrabe.

E. B. White's classic young adult novel *Charlotte's Web* (1952) tells the story of a young pig, Wilbur, befriended and saved from the butcher's block by Charlotte, an intelligent spider. Charlotte spins messages in her web to convince their farmer that Wilbur is too special to become bacon; in the process, she also boosts Wilbur's confidence in himself. "When Charlotte's web said SOME PIG, Wilbur tried hard to look like some pig. When Charlotte's web said TERRIFIC, Wilbur had tried to look terrific. And now that the web said RADIANT, he did everything possible to make himself glow."

Crome Yellow (1922) author Aldous Huxley skillfully depicts a mother sow who'd just given birth to a litter of fourteen:

> "Fourteen?" Mary echoed incredulously. She turned astonished blue eyes toward Mr. Wimbush, then let them fall on to the seething mass of *élan vital* that fermented in the sty.
>
> An immense sow reposed on her side in the middle of the pen. Her round, black belly, fringed with a double line of dugs, presented itself to the assault of an army of small, brownish-black swine. With a frantic greed they tugged at their mother's flank. The old sow stirred sometimes uneasily or uttered a little grunt of pain. One small pig, the runt, the weakling of the litter, had been unable to secure a place at the banquet. Squealing shrilly, he ran backwards and forwards, trying to push in among his stronger brothers or even to climb over their tight little black backs toward the maternal reservoir. . . .

The value of the family pig and its litter are depicted in the book *Lark Rise to Candleford* (1945), by Flora Thompson:

> During its lifetime the pig was an important member of the family, and its health and condition were regularly reported in letters to children away from home, together with news of their brothers and sisters. Men callers on Sunday afternoons came, not to see the family, but the pig, and would lounge with its owner against the pigsty door for an hour, scratching piggy's back and praising his points or turning up their noses in criticism. Ten to fifteen shillings was the price paid for a pigling when weaned, and they all delighted in getting a bargain. Some men swore by the "dilling," as the smallest of a litter was called, saying it was little and good, and would soon catch up; others preferred to give a few shillings more for a larger younger pig.

Lewis Carroll describes another kind of baby pig (or pig-baby) in *Alice's Adventures in Wonderland* (1866):

> "Don't grunt," said Alice; "that's not at all a proper way of expressing yourself." The baby grunted again, and Alice looked very anxiously into its face to see what was the matter with it. There could be no doubt that it had a *very* turn up nose, much more like a snout than a real nose; also its eyes

Whose little pigs are these, these, these?
Whose little pigs are these?
They are Roger the Cook's, I know by their looks;
I found them among my peas.
Go pound them, go pound them.
I dare not on my life.
For though I love not Roger the Cook,
I dearly love his wife.
—Traditional
(Photograph © Alan and Sandy Carey)

Pig Riddles
Now in one body I have twice six eyes
And twice three heads, but all my other parts
Rule these. Upborne on twice two feet I walk,
And yet my body's nails are ninety-six.
In number like a metric syzygy
I thus appear. The poplar and the yew
And green-leaved tree I hate, but love
The crooked beech-tree with its nuts, and oaks
With thick-crowned head that juicy acorns bear,
Nor do I scorn the holm-oak with its shade.
Answer: A pregnant sow.
—from St. Aldhelm of Malmesbury, (D. 709), Bishop of Sherborne
and Abbot of Malmesbury, in *Epistola ad Acircium*

were getting extremely small for a baby; altogether Alice did not like the look of the thing at all. "But perhaps it was only sobbing," she thought, and looked into its eyes again to see if there were any tears.

No, there were no tears. "If you're going to turn into a pig, my dear," said Alice, seriously, "I'll have nothing more to do with you. Mind now!" The poor little thing sobbed again (or grunted, it was impossible to say which) and they went on for some while in silence.

P. G. Wodehouse is more flattering, describing a pig named "The Empress of Blandings" in his 1952 book, *Pigs Have Wings*:

There was only one thing to be done, if he hoped to recover calm of spirit. He straightened his pince-nez, and went off to the piggeries to have a look at Empress of Blandings . . .

The Empress lived in a bijou residence not far from the kitchen garden, and when Lord Emsworth arrived at her boudoir she was engaged, as pretty nearly always when you dropped in on her, in hoisting into her vast interior whose fifty-seven thousand and eight hundred calories on which Whiffle insists . . .

The Empress uttered a plaintive grunt. A potato, full of calories, had detached itself from the rest of her ration and rolled outside the sty. Gally returned it courteously, and the noble animal thanked him with a brief snuffle.

In her novel *Moo* (1995), American author Jane Smiley provides a pig's-eye point of view of this appetite with this description of Earl Butz, a hog kept for research purposes at the book's fictional university:

Earl Butz was getting monstrous big. Earl himself felt it in the effort it took him to heave himself to his trotters in the morning, in his increasing desire to lie around and have things, like cooling baths, brought to him, rather than going out to receive them. . . . He still worked hard at his main occupation of eating. He couldn't help that, it was bred into him; but like any variety of genius, appetite was beginning to overshadow other, more individual traits of his personality.

And, finally, the *coup de grace*: Victor Hugo, in *les Miserables* (1862) defines a degree of drunkenness so disgusting he can only describe it in terms of swine:

Upon the first goblet he read this inscription, *monkey wine*; upon the second, *lion wine*; upon the third, *sheep wine*; upon the fourth, *swine wine*. These four inscriptions expressed the four descending degrees of drunkenness: the first, that which enlivens; the second, that which irritates; the third, that which stupefies; finally the last, that which brutalizes.

The innate intelligence of the hog, however, has not been entirely overlooked. In *Animal Farm* (1945), George Orwell celebrates their intellectual eminence:

Alice in Wonderland
Illustration drawn by John Tenniel for the book by Lewis Carroll (1865). "Alice was just beginning to think to herself, 'Now, what am I to do with this creature when I get it home?' when it grunted again, so violently, that she looked down into its face in some alarm. This time there could be *no* mistake about it; it was neither more nor less than a pig and she felt that it would be quite absurd for her to carry it any further. . . ."

Happy as a pig in mud
Ah! "To be happy as a pig in mud" is to be very happy, indeed. But pigs don't wallow in puddles merely to get dirty; pigs have no sweat glands, and the cool mud helps to lower their body temperature in warm weather. (Photograph © Lynn M. Stone)

"One disadvantage of being a hog is that at any moment some blundering fool may try to make a silk purse out of your wife's ear."
—J. B. Morton ("Beachcomer"), *By The Way* (1931)

"Tom, Tom, the Piper's Son"
Illustration from *Twilight Stories* (1905).

The work of teaching and organizing the others fell naturally upon the pigs, who were generally recognized as being the cleverest of animals. Pre-eminent among the pigs were two young boars named Snowball and Napoleon, whom Mr. Jones was breeding for sale. Napoleon was a large, rather fierce-looking Berkshire boar, the only Berkshire on the farm, not much of a talker, but with a reputation for getting his own way. Snowball was a more vivacious pig than Napoleon, quicker in speech and more inventive, but was not considered to have the same depth of character. All the other male pigs on the farm were porkers. The best known among them was a small fat pig named Squealer, with very round cheeks, twinkling eyes, nimble movements, and a shrill voice. He was a brilliant talker, and when he was arguing some difficult point he had a way of skipping from side to side and whisking his tail which was somehow very persuasive.

William Golding places a group of boys on an island in *Lord of the Flies* (1959). As a reflection, perhaps, on the role of the pig in ancient sacrificial ceremonies, the boys offer up a pig's head to the unknown menace that they sense there:

He paused and stood up, looking at the shadows under the trees. His voice was lower when he spoke again.

"But we'll leave part of the kill for . . ."

He knelt down again and was busy with his knife. The boys crowded round him. He spoke over his shoulder to Roger.

"Sharpen a stick at both ends."

Presently he stood up, holding the dripping sow's head in his hands.

"Where's that stick?"

"Here."

"Ram one end in the earth. Oh—it's rock. Jam it in that crack. There."

Jack held up the head and jammed the soft throat down on the pointed end of the stick which pierced through into the mouth. He stood back and the head hung there, a little blood dribbling down the stick.

Instinctively the boys drew back too; and the forest was very still. They listened, and the loudest noise was the buzzing of flies over the spilled guts.

Jack spoke in a whisper.

"Pick up the pig."

Maurice and Robert skewered the carcass, lifted the dead weight, and stood ready. In the silence, and standing over the dry blood, they looked suddenly furtive.

Jack spoke loudly.

"This head is for the beast. It's a gift."

The silence accepted the gift and awed them. The head remained there, dim-eyed, grinning faintly, blood blackening between the teeth. All at once they were running away, as fast as they could, through the forest towards the open beach.

Thomas Hardy expresses deep compassion for his character, Jude, when he had to butcher the family hog, a task for which poor Jude was ill-suited:

The time arrived for killing the pig which Jude and his wife had fattened in their sty during the autumn

What is the marvel that I have seen outside Delling's doorway?
This creature has ten tongues, twenty eyes, forty feet, and walks with difficulty.
Answer: A sow with nine piglets.
—from *The Hervarar Saga,* an ancient Icelandic saga, in the story of Heidrek and Riddles of Gestumblindi (circa 1325)

Pigling Bland
Cover illustration from *The Tale of Pigling Bland,* by Beatrix Potter (1913). Miss Potter's fictional pigs led a playful, gentle life compared to those on her own farm, where, she admitted, "they led prosperous uneventful lives, and their end was bacon." (© Frederick Warne & Co., 1913, 1987)

Foppish pig

Foppish pig, drawing from *A Tale in Five Curls*, published 1880. The little pig who once cried "Wee wee wee, all the way home" became "a rather fat lad, who, I am sorry to say, is very much averse to work, and spends his time in strutting about the place dressed up in gorgeous style, with short jacket and low shoes, a hat on his head, and a cane umbrella under his arm, a sort of foppish pig, doing nothing."

A little pig found a fifty-dollar note,
And purchased a hat and a very fine coat,
With trousers, and stockings, and shoes,
    Cravat, and shirt-collar, and
        gold-headed cane,
Then proud as could be, did he march
        up the lane,
    Says he, "I shall hear all the news."
        —Mother Goose rhyme

---

months, and the butchering was timed to take place as soon as it was light in the morning . . . But it had snowed overnight, and the pig-killer did not arrive as scheduled. Jude and his wife had run out of food for the hog, so there was no choice: They had to kill the pig themselves. Jude was reluctant, and his wife called him a tender-hearted fool.

"Upon my soul, I would sooner have gone without the pig than have had this to do!," said Jude. "A creature I have fed with my own hands."

Pigs in Children's Literature

Little Betty Pringle she had a pig,
It was not very little and not very
    big;
When he was alive he lived in clover
But now he's dead and that's all
    over.
Johnny Pringle he sat down and
    cried,
Betty Pringle she lay down and died;
So there was an end of one, two,
    three,
Johnny Pringle he,
Betty Pringle she
And piggy Wiggy.
    —Mother Goose rhyme

Pigs have inhabited children's nurseries for hundreds of years, tickling their fancies with nonsense rhymes and adventures that often stress good moral values.

Tom, Tom the piper's son,
He learned to play when he was
    young.
But all the tune that he could play
Was "Over the hills and far away."

Tom, Tom, the piper's son
Stole a pig and away he run;
The pig was eat, and Tom was beat,
And Tom went howling down the
    street.

British children may have preferred *The Tale of Pigling Bland* (1913) to all other pig stories. Beatrix Potter writes of two little pigs, Pigling and his brother, Alexander, who are sent off to market one day. But Alexander fools around and his papers get mislaid, so he is taken home in disgrace by a policeman. Pigling finds Alexander's papers but gets hopelessly lost in his excitement. Eventually he meets up with the charming Pig-wig, "a perfectly lovely little black Berkshire pig with twinkly little screwed up eyes, a double chin, and a short turned-up nose," who shares his peppermints and agrees to escape with him "over the hills and far away." Many years after the publication of *The Tale of Pigling Bland*, Potter wrote a second book with a pig as the lead character, *Little Pig Robinson*, but it was not as popular.

In the popular tale "The Three Little Pigs," said pigs go off into the world to seek their fortunes. The first two pigs, who build flimsy houses of straw and sticks, are gobbled up by the Big Bad Wolf. The third little pig patiently builds a sturdy house of bricks and outsmarts the beast who ends up in a boiling pot. In the 1970s, educators feared that children would suffer psychological harm in learning the fate of the first two pigs, but Bruno Bettelheim, in *The Uses of Enchantment* (1977), insists that fairy tales comforted children by ministering to the infant unconscious. Bettelheim also claims, "The houses the three pigs build are symbolic of man's progress in history: from a lean-to shack to a wooden house, finally to a house of solid brick."

The symbolism was not as clear cut in the poem-story, *The Old Woman and Her Pig*:

An old woman was sweeping her house, and she found a little crooked sixpence. "What," said she, "shall I do with this little sixpence? I will go to market and buy a little pig." As she was coming home, she came to a stile: The piggy would not go over the stile.
   She went a little further, and she met a dog. So she said to the dog—
"Dog, dog, bite pig;
Piggy won't get over the stile;
And I shan't get home to-night. . . ."

Of course, this is an invitation for many more animals to come along and encourage Piggy to move his curly tail up and over the stile, which he eventually does.

Here are some more examples of nursery rhymes that feature pigs.

To market, to market, to buy a fat
   pig
Home again, home again, jiggety-jig
To market to market to buy a fat
   hog,
Home again, home again, jiggety
   jog.

As I went to Bonner
I met a pig
Without a wig,
Upon my word and honour.

Barber, barber, shave a pig.
How many hairs will make a wig?

Four and twenty, that's enough.
Give the poor barber a pinch of
   snuff.

This reference, to "shave a pig," has been suggested by scholars to refer to "doing something not worth doing."

Jack Sprat's pig
He was not very little
Nor yet very big;
He was not very lean,
He was not very fat.
He'll do well for a grunt,
Says little Jack Sprat.

Pig afield
Hamilton, the "ball-pig" and mascot for the Saint Paul (Minnesota) Saints minor-league baseball team, carries new baseballs in his vest pockets from the home-plate umpire to the pitcher. The Saints have had a pig mascot since 1993, the team's inaugural season. Each year a new piglet is chosen for that prestigious role. (Photograph © 1999 by the Saint Paul Saints)

117

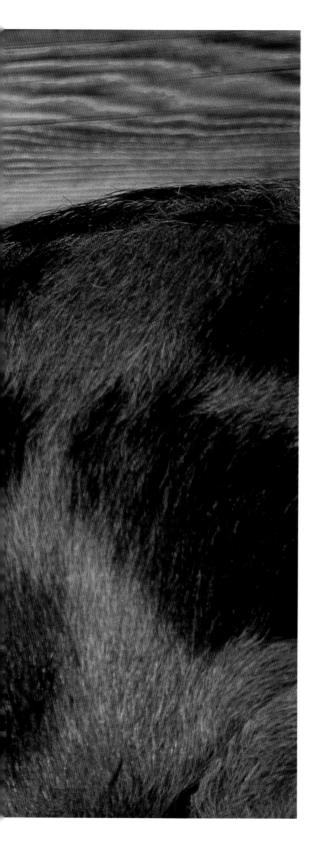

When Pigs Fly

Dickery, dickery, dare,
The pig flew up in the air:
The man in brown soon brought him
down
Dickery, dickery, dare.
—Children's nursery rhyme

In 1553, *A Short Dictionarie for Younge Begynners* confidently proclaimed, "Pigs flie in the ayre with their tails forward...." That was amended, in the 1620s, to read, "Pigs might fly, but they are very unlike birds," a euphemism popular at the time.

Perhaps due to the ludicrous image it conjures, the concept of a flying pig has excited the imagination of would-be pig lovers for centuries. In A. A. Milne's 1928 book, Winnie the Pooh asks Owl if he could "fly up to the letter-box with Piglet on your back," to which Piglet abruptly responds, "He couldn't," perhaps aware of the temerity of becoming an actual flying pig.

A pig did take off into the wild blue yonder in 1909 with Lord Brabazon, holder of the first pilot's license in Britain; the piglet was tucked inside a basket tied to the plane's wing with a sign attached announcing, "I am the first pig to fly."

Further flying pig sightings, however, have been limited. Nevertheless, pigs continue to perform astonishing feats that have amazed one and all with their innate intelligence, endurance, and capacity to entertain and amuse.

"I have myself a poetical enthusiasm for pigs," author G. K. Chesterton admitted in 1923, "And the paradise of my fancy is one where pigs have wings. But it is only men, especially wise men, who discuss whether pigs can fly; we have no particular proof that pigs ever discuss it."

Flying pigs obviously piqued the curiosity of *Alice in Wonderland* author Lewis Carroll. He brought up the questionable concept in his poem, *The Walrus and the Carpenter*:

"The time has come," the Walrus said,
"To talk of many things:
Of shoes—and ships—and sealing-wax—
Of cabbages and kings—
And why the sea is boiling hot—
And whether pigs have wings."

Peek-a-boo
A young piglet hides from his littermates behind his mother's healthy haunches. (Photograph © Alan and Sandy Carey)

A long tail'd Pig, or a short tail'd
  Pig,
Or a Pig without any Tail;
A Sow Pig, or a Boar Pig,
Or a Pig with a curling Tail.
Take hold of the Tail and eat off his
  Head;
And then you'll be sure the Pig hog
  is dead.

The last verse was the cry of the eighteenth century "Pig Pye Men," who sold pastry pigs (made with two currants for eyes) in the streets of English cities. In fact, this is the kind of pig supposedly stolen by Tom Tom the Piper's Son, who "Stole a pig and away he run."

Precocious Performing Porkers

"Learned pigs" was the first term used to describe the trained pig who appeared on the British stage in late 1783. Trained by Mr. S. Bisset, a Scottish shoemaker who had already trained dogs, horses, and monkeys, the black suckling pig underwent sixteen months of training before exhibiting his repertoire of tricks: solving math problems, spelling names, telling time, "reading" flashcards for the audience. Unfortunately, a local official, incensed with the display of porcine perspicacity, interrupted a subsequent show, beat Bissit, and threatened to kill his learned pig.

Bisset died not long afterward from an illness associated with the attack, but the pig went on to become—scholars believe—the same learned pig advertised in 1785 as "The Amazing Learned Pig," and shown by Mr. Nicholson at Scarborough and York. The pig performed similar feats in company with a rabbit that beat a drum and a turtle that was trained to fetch. An article in the *Daily Universal Register* (1785) enthusiastically declared, "This entertaining and sagacious Animal casts accounts by means of Typographical cards, in the same manner as a Printer composes; and by the same method sets down any Capital or Surname, reckons the number of People present, tells by evoking on a Gentleman's Watch in company what is the Hour and Minutes; he likewise tells any Lady's Thoughts in Company and distinguishes all sorts of colours."

A less sanguine reviewer called it "a very ridiculous show. . . . The *pig*, which indeed was a large, unwieldy *hog*, being taught to pick up letters written upon pieces of cards, and to arrange them at command, gave great satisfaction to all who saw him, and filled his tormentor's purse with money."

Naturally, competition arose. "The Amazing Pig of Knowledge" was able to select playing cards while blindfolded. Meanwhile, the original "Learned Pig" suffered humiliation when his second owner, Mr. Nicholson, was "confined in a madhouse in Edinburgh. Too much learning we suppose had driven the pig mad, so he bit his master!" The pig then suffered even greater ignominy, although his obituary claimed he made more money "than any other actor or actress within the same compass of time."

In 1797, "The PIG of KNOWLEDGE!!" made his debut on the American stage, in New York and Boston. This pig, whose ownership and training were attributed to William Frederick Pinchbeck, published a manual for pig-training in 1805 called *The Expositor: or Many*

Felix Adler and friend

A beloved clown with Ringling Brothers & Barnum and Bailey Circus for fifty years, Felix Adler was famous for the trained piglets he included in his act. But each baby pig outgrew its role after only a few weeks on the road, so Adler frequently left them with friendly folks he met along the circus's route. (Circus World Museum, Baraboo, Wisconsin)

In the late nineteenth century, the city of Cincinnati, Ohio, became known as a center of pork production, earning itself the nickname "Porkopolis." In 1833, Cincinnati slaughtered or packed 85,000 hogs. That number grew to 360,000 hogs in 1853, and ten years later, during the Civil War, 608,457 hogs were slaughtered and processed there, shipped out of the city by means of the Ohio River. Citizens of that city proudly proclaimed they had "originated and perfected the system which packs fifteen bushels of corn into a pig, and packs that pig into a barrel, and sends him over the mountains and over the ocean to feed mankind."

Others did not find the city's claim to fame as praiseworthy. English novelist Frances Milton Trollope visited Cincinnati in 1827 as part of an American tour, and her view of the city was less than flattering, as she writes in her book *Domestic Manners of Americans* (1832).

I am sure I should have liked Cincinnati much better if the people had not dealt so very largely in hogs! The immense quantity of business done in this line would hardly be believed by those who had not witnessed it. . . . If I determined upon a walk up Main Street, the chances were five hundred to one against my reaching the shady side without brushing by a snout or two, fresh dripping from the kennel. When we had screwed up our courage to the enterprise of mounting a certain noble-looking sugarloaf hill, that promised pure air and a fine view, we found the brook we had to cross at its foot red with the blood from a pig slaughterhouse; while our noses, instead of meeting 'the thyme that loves the green hill's breast' were greeted by odours that I will not describe, and which I heartily hope my readers cannot imagine; our feet, that on leaving the city had expected to press the flowery sod, literally got entangled in pigs' tails and jaw-bones; and thus the prettiest walk in the neighbourhood was interdicted for ever.

In the twentieth century, Cincinnati's pork processing production declined. The city's

Logo of Cincinnati's Flying Pig Marathon
The popularity of the city's flying pigs reached new heights in May 1999 with the first annual Cincinnati Flying Pig Marathon. Organizers chose the name to tie the event into the city's history and give the race an aura of fun. More than six thousand runners participated in the marathon in its first year, and organizers attribute the event's success, in part, to its creative name. (Courtesy of the Cincinnati Flying Pig Marathon)

reputation as Porkopolis might have been quietly forgotten, if not for a public sculpture commissioned to celebrate Cincinnati's bicentennial in 1988.

Although the flying pigs were just one aspect of the larger work, critics complained that including the swine in the commemorative sculpture would be embarrassing, even insulting, to the city. Pig proponents countered that the flying pigs were a whimsical representation of Cincinnati's history. Finally, after months of polls, press coverage, and public debate, Leicester's pigs were allowed to fly. Called the Cincinnati Gateway, the pigs and the sculpture are located in Bicentennial Commons, the park along the city's riverfront.

Since the Gateway was dedicated in June 1988, the flying pigs have become an increasingly visible symbol in Cincinnati, with flying pig merchandise available at stores throughout the city.

Flying pigs
Flying pig sculpture, perched above the Cincinnati Gateway. Realizing that pigs played a crucial part in the city's early history, artist Andrew Leicester incorporated four flying pigs into his design for the commemorative sculpture. He says the winged swine represent "the angelic spirits" of all the pigs who were slaughtered for the prosperity of the city." (Photograph and artwork © Andrew Leicester)

Porky Pig

Warner Bros.'s animated character Porky Pig went through various looks before becoming the well-known face he is today. (© 1989 Warner Bros. All Rights Reserved.)

Mysteries Unravelled, which began by advising that a seven- or eight-week-old piglet "have free access to the inferior part of your house until he shall become in some measure domesticated."

Toby was the name of the next pig to take London by storm. Known by the stage name of Toby the Sapient Porker, he was declared able to "Discover a Person's Thoughts, a Thing never heard of before to be exhibited by an Animal of the SWINE RACE." Toby subsequently "wrote" a pamphlet entitled *The Life and Adventures of Toby the Sapient Pig: With Opinions of Men and Manners* (circa 1817), in which he, the "first of my race that ever wielded a pen," gave an account of his training and claimed his name came from his master's recitation of Hamlet's soliloquy, "To be or not to be."

Whether it was or was not ("to be or not to be"), *Toby* became the generic name for any trained pig, and many more Tobys appeared, some in troupes that performed acrobatic routines and others in the company of clowns. In the United States, similar "learned pigs" toured the country, and were exhibited at taverns and wagon stands.

In his book, *Learned Pigs & Fireproof Women* (1987), Ricky Jay explains that the problem with training pigs is not their capacity to learn, for they are intelligent animals and easily trained; the difficulty is that pigs physically outgrow their routine.

"Such was the case with Fred Leslie," Jay reports, "whose 'Porcine Circus' worked the Lemen Brothers Show around the turn of the century. When his star pigs grew too large to perform their acrobatics gracefully, he purchased a new group of shoats to take their place. The newcomers watched the old troupers and were trained to do the act. When the youngsters were ready to perform, Leslie sold the fattened veterans to a farmer whose land bordered the circus lot. That evening, as the music for the show began, the old-timers recognized their cue and, using their ladder-scaling prowess, climbed over the farmer's fence and made their way into the circus tent in time for their act to begin. The image of them nudging the rookie pigs out of carts, away from seesaws, and off ladders in an attempt to do their old routine is a testament to the finest traditions of show business."

Given their success on the stage, it is no surprise that the versatile pig has proven itself to be well suited for other entertainment media.

Hollywood has not been immune to the pig's charisma, and swine have had prominent roles in films, television shows, and animated cartoons.

Actual sights of snouts and sounds of snorts and snuffles arrived in Tinseltown when Will Rogers starred in the 1933 movie *State Fair* with "Blue Boy," a Hampshire, who was really the star of the show.

Animated hero Porky Pig made his debut in Fritz Freleng's 1935 cartoon "I Haven't Got a Hat." One of many animated characters that Warner Bros. was testing in a sort of "Our Gang" setting at that time, the very first Porky was so rotund he was practically a complete circle. Porky was a hit, but for a while his identity changed from picture to picture. The character achieved his first coherent personna when director Bob Clampett

Three Little Pigs
Walt Disney's animated version of the "Three Little Pigs," featuring Fiddler Pig, Fifer Pig, and Practical Pig, was released in 1933. (© Disney Enterprises, Inc.)

Piggly Wiggly ®, founded in Memphis, Tennessee in 1916 by Clarence Saunders, was America's first true self-service grocery store. Up until that time, shoppers had to present their orders to clerks who ran around the grocery store, gathering their goods. Saunders came up with the idea of open shelves and shopping carts, and he also came up with the name, "Piggly Wiggly." But Saunders was reluctant to reveal his reasons for choosing that name. When asked, he would always reply, "So people will ask that very question."

Pumbaa

"You can't go wrong with a pig"—even if your story is set on the African plains, as is *The Lion King* (Walt Disney Pictures, 1994). In this animated tale, the pig in question is a funny, flatulent wart hog named Pumbaa. (© Disney Enterprises, Inc.)

"I was very disturbed when Jesus found a demon in a guy and He put the demon into a herd of pigs, then sent them off a cliff. What did the pigs do? I could never figure that out. It just seemed very un-Christian."
—Matt Groening, creator of *The Simpsons*

Hog Calling

In ancient Italy, swineherds separated their swine from enormous droves by blasting a sound on the horn whose notes the swine recognized as their own. Nowadays, hog calling is claimed by many to be an exclusively American skill, initially celebrated at the "Century of Progress" in 1933 and 1934 when the magazine *Prairie Journal* and Chicago radio station WLS sponsored a competition for all-American Hog Calling Championship. Just as the "fattest hog contest" and "greased hog race" continue in popularity, hog calling contests still take place at county fairs around the United States.

Hog callers are graded on points for:
• Strength of tone (must be able to be heard across a forty-acre field of clover);
• Quality of tone (must seem friendly and welcoming to the hog);
• Originality of call (the hog knows the call is meant especially for him or her);
• Persuasiveness or appeal of the call (in case the hog is temporarily engaged in a meal of acorns or other good stuff);
• Variety (Since the hog is a creature of delicate moods and temperament, and prone to boredom, it is important to express variety).

Missouri hog callers favor a long, drawn-out "Who-o-oey," but "So-o-oey" (derived from the Latin word for pig) is most popular in other places. Also heard is "Hy-y-aa," and "P-e-eg, P-e-eg."

Arnold Ziffel
Arnold Ziffel, seen here with co-stars Eva Gabor and Eddie Arnold, stole the show on TV's *Green Acres*. Here they were filming the episode "Guess Who's Coming to the Luau." (CBS Photo Archive)

Circus poster (1898)
Not only could trained pigs read thoughts, tell fortunes, or play musical instruments; their repertoire might include such acrobatic stunts as climbing ladders, rolling hoops, pushing carriages, walking on tightropes, balancing on a see-saw, and pulling a cart that was driven by a dog. (Library of Congress)

restyled his body and personality in the late 1930s. In the 1940s, enhanced with Mel Blanc's inimitable stutter, Porky Pig became the star of Looney Tunes. He was eventually given a girlfriend, Petunia, and his famous line at the close of Looney Tunes cartoons, "Th-th-th-that's all, folks!" will live on forevermore.

Another animated hero, Napoleon, was the star of the 1954 British film based on George Orwell's *Animal Farm*. Most of the pig supporting characters exhibited stereotypical pig characteristics as they formed a police state and took over the management of their farm.

Talk about animated! One cannot possibly ignore Miss Piggy, for her flamboyant glamour and sultry beauty have carried her far beyond the chorus line of her inauspicious origin as a mere backup singer on Jim Henson's television program *The Muppet Show*, which debuted in 1976. Miss Piggy went on to star in four feature films and authored a best-selling book on beauty and fashion, *Miss Piggy's Guide To Life* (as told to Henry Beard, 1981).

Arnold Ziffel was an actual pig, a Chester White born in Indiana, who starred in the CBS-TV sitcom, *Green Acres*. Arnold was trained by Hollywood animal trainer Frank Inn. His first appearance

Casting Call
Eager to hog the limelight, these little porkers display their best side. (Photograph © Jim Steinbacher, courtesy of Leslie Levy Creative Art Licensing, Scottsdale, AZ)

The first pig to appear on radio was Spammy, who debuted on George and Gracie Allen's radio show in 1941 as a "spokespig" for their sponsor SPAM.

on *Green Acres* was in 1965, in an episode in which he played the piano. During Arnold's years on the show he opened doors, fetched the mail, opened a refrigerator to remove food, watched TV westerns, and stole the show from his co-stars, Eddie Arnold and Eva Gabor. "Nobody cared if I'd powdered my nose," Gabor complained, "When the pig was ready, we began shooting. In a sense it was most humiliating to share billing with a pig, but who wants to fight success?"

For two years running (1968 and 1969), Arnold Ziffel was named Performing Animal Television Star of the Year, and he earned $250 per day. Unfortunately, as soon as the original Arnold topped ninety pounds and aged a bit he was replaced by one of his doubles, a younger and sleeker understudy. Sorry to say, the original Arnold suffered an incongruous fate: As with most pigs, Arnold was butchered and intended for his animal trainer's plate. Meanwhile, however, pork from Arnold was stored in Frank Inn's freezer and—oh! the indignity!—the power went off, and the pork that was Arnold Ziffel eventually spoiled and had to be discarded.

A hilarious British film, *A Private Function*, written by Alan Bennett and directed by Malcom Mowbray, appeared in 1984. The HandMade Films production starred Michael Palin, Maggie Smith, and Denholm Elliott. The comedy satirized the efforts of a small British community to fatten a pig during the time following World War II when, due to a shortage of supply, ham was deemed contraband.

The introduction to the published screenplay by Bennett recounts Palin's experience when he attempts to kidnap the pig: "With one trotter in his crotch and the other around his neck, Michael Palin compared it to being in a car with an overweight and over-amorous landlady. And like landladies they are, trotting naked over the linoleum in their little high heels, delicate and fastidious, their quivering bottoms wonderful to see."

And then there's *Babe*, a 1995 production of Universal Studios directed by George Miller. The movie was an adaptation of the 1985 children's book by Dick King-Smith about "a pig with an unprejudiced heart." Fifty female piglets were used to portray the first Babe (because male genitals would look unseemly, reported a November 1998 article in the *New Yorker*). When the piglets had grown too large, they were given to folks who signed agreements that the little animals would not be slaughtered.

With the 1998 sequel, *Babe: Pig in the City*, four-week-old piglets were chosen for their liveliness and charisma, and they were trained for ten weeks. Alas, each "Babe" could be onscreen for only three weeks before she outgrew her role. The magazine reported that each day the working pigs would each be "washed and made up, their eyelashes dyed black, and their distinctive, tufty toupees, which Miller designed, glued in place." Director Miller says that he sees Babe as the classical mythical hero, "an agent of change who relinquishes self-interest and breaks down the established social order."

The Lyrical Pig

Musicians have not been able to escape the charms of the beloved pig, and many songwriters have paid tribute to pigs in their lyrics.

Singing Pigs

Louis XI of France, also known as "The Cruel," was a fifteenth-century monarch known for "caprices and humours which were very singular." In fact, his melancholy could only be cheered by a troop of pigs, dressed in clothes and wigs. One folly involved Louis XI and the Abbot of Baigne, an inventor of musical instruments. "The Cruel" Louis asked the Abbot to build an instrument like an organ consisting of a collection of pigs of assorted ages and "voices," hidden beneath a velvet coverlet. Next to this he placed a table and a keyboard arrangement that, when the keys were pressed, pricked the pigs with little spikes and made them call out in a particular order, thus pleasing the King and certainly annoying the pigs.

This may have been the origin of the maxim, "Never try to teach a pig to sing; you'll only waste your time, and annoy the pig."

Porcine trio
Under your mighty ancestors, we pigs
Were blessed as nightingales on myrtle sprigs,
Or grass-hoppers that live on noon-day dew
And sung, old annals tell, as sweetly too . . .
—"Oedipus Tyrannus," Percy Bysshe Shelley
(Photograph © Alan and Sandy Carey)

Big pigs
Kansas-reared Poland Chinas resemble hilarious overstuffed sausages in this illustration from F. D. Coburn's *Swine in America* (1816).

Dave Goulder's folksong "Pigs Can See the Wind," from his *Harbors of Home* album (1998), recalls the superstition that pigs have the ability to forecast the weather:

My father used to say to me
as he locked 'em in the sty
They say that pigs can see the wind
and I'm going to tell you why . . .

Chorus:
Well the summer may come
and the summer may go
And the pigs can see the wind.
The autumn goose brings down the
 snow
and the pigs can see the wind.

Native Iowan Greg Brown has fun with his tune "Four Wet Pigs," on his album *The Iowa Waltz* (1981):

Here's a little song about four wet
 pigs
Two are little & two are big

They're all dancing at the mudtime
 jig. . . .
Cut 'em into bacon. Slice 'em into
 ham
Chop 'em into hotdogs. Squeeze 'em
 into Spam. . . .

The *Folksinger's Wordbook* (1973) features words and chords for more than a thousand songs, including "The Sow Took the Measles," written by an anonymous composer:

How do you think I began in the
 world?
I got me a sow and sev'ral other
 things.
The sow took the measles and she
 died in the spring.
What do you think I made of her
 hide?
The very best saddle that you ever
 did ride.
Saddle or bridle or any such thing.
The sow took the measles and she
 died in the spring. . . .

An oft-quoted pig-song, sometimes called "The Irish Pig," was composed by Benjamin Hapgood Burt in 1933 and entitled "The Pig Got Up and Slowly Walked Away":

One evening in October, when I was
 one-third sober,
An' taking home a "load" with
 manly pride;
My poor feet began to stutter, so I
 lay down in the gutter,
And a pig came up an' lay down by
 my side
Then we sang "It's all fair weather
 when good fellows get together,"

Cow in disguise

Sculpture "The Cow (in Disguise)," by artist John Loftus was on display as part of Chicago's 1999 "Cows on Parade" public art exhibit. (Photograph and artwork © John Loftus)

Till a lady passing by was heard to say:

"You can tell a man who boozes by the company he chooses"

And the pig got up and slowly walked away.

Pigs in Art

Moonbeam McSwine, daughter of Big Barnsmell (created by Al Capp for his comic strip *Li'l Abner*) is a difficult work of pig art to define, except that she *was* a McSwine. One senses, however, that Capp did not require weeks in the sty to capture the image of Moonbeam. Such was not the case with other artists who chose to paint the pig.

Beatrix Potter, author and illustrator of *The Tale of Pigling Bland* and *Little Pig Robinson*, lived on a farm in the Lake District of England where she raised pigs. In 1910, she wrote to a little girl in New Zealand, "I think I shall put *myself* in the next book. It will be about pigs; I shall put in me walking about with my old 'Goosey' sow; she is such a pet."

"Portrait of Pig"
Artist Jamie Wyeth painted a four-by-seven-foot portrait of his 450-pound Yorkshire sow named Den-Den. According to William Hedgepeth, author of *The Hog Book* (1978), Wyeth became "purely enamored" of Den-Den because her eyes were "so human . . . like a Kennedy's." During the portrait-sitting, however, Den-Den consumed seventeen tubes of oil paint and for weeks thereafter left rainbow droppings in her wake. ("Portrait of Pig" © Jamie Wyeth, 1970)

"The brain of this foolish-compounded clay, man, is not able to invent anything that tends to laughter, more than invent or is invented on me: I am not only witty in myself, but the cause that wit is in other men. I do here walk before thee like a sow that hath overwhelmed all her litter but one."
—William Shakespeare, *Henry IV, Part 2* (1597)

One Potter biography, *The Tale of Beatrix Potter* (1982) by Margaret Lane, discusses the way in which living on a farm affected Potter's work: "She was interested, in particular, in drawing her pigs, and from time to time added to the sketches which later were to form the basis of *Pigling Bland*. 'I have done a little sketching when it does not rain, and I spent a very wet hour *inside* the pig-sty drawing the pig. It tries to nibble my boots, which is interrupting.' 'I was rather overdone with the head yesterday,' she wrote, after drawing and modelling a suckling pig which had been killed for Christmas. 'The poor little cherub had such a sweet smile, but in other respects it was disagreeable. It is rather a shame to kill them so young; one has no sentimental feelings about a large bacon pig.'"

The only hint of a self-portrait in any Potter's books is in *The Tale of Pigling Bland*, where we find the sentence "'I pinned the papers, for safety, inside their waistcoat pockets,'" and see a simple sketch of a woman attending a small pig.

Potter's pigs, as those with most artists who illustrate childrens' books, are imaginative, wear clothing, walk on their hind feet, and usually speak. Artists such as Rembrandt, Rubens, Dürer, and Gainsborough endeavored to capture and depict the natural charm of pigs without the benefit of attributing human characteristics.

There is a wall-painting from the mid–first century B.C. in the Villa of the Mysteries, Pompeii, that features a fat black pig with a bright red ribbon, a "dorsuale," tied around its belly, that indicates he is going to be sacrificed to Priapus, the god of male potency. It is suspected that the painting has a male homosexual theme, mainly because of where it is located in relation to other paintings in the room.

Artistic representations are also found in illuminations of mediaeval manuscripts and in wooden church carvings all over England and Ireland where pigs are found carved and molded in abbeys, churches, and cathedrals, playing musical instruments and in various attitudes—evidence of the animals' high place in people's affections.

Political Pigs

You wouldn't expect to find pigs in politics, but Pigasus was the first and only pig to run for President of the United States. During the Democratic National Convention held in Chicago in 1968, Abbie Hoffman and other Yippie protest organizers known as the Chicago Seven conducted antiwar demonstrations against the Vietnam war. One of their stunts involved the nomination of Pigasus. Hoffman found a pig and brought it downtown to participate in the protest but the police began making arrests when the crowd started singing "The Star-Spangled Banner" in homage to the pig. According to Stew Albert, one of the Chicago Seven, the group was in jail when a policeman appeared and said, "I have bad news for you boys. The pig squealed." Albert said, "That was the best cop joke I ever heard."

How to draw a pig
Because its distinctive snout, the pig is easy to draw. It's essentially an oval with a snout and a curly tail. (Drawing © Jay Rath)

"No man should be allowed to be the President who does not understand hogs, or hasn't been around a manure pile."
—Harry S. Truman (1884–1972)
Kansas farmer and thirty-third
President of the United States

135

Greased Pigs

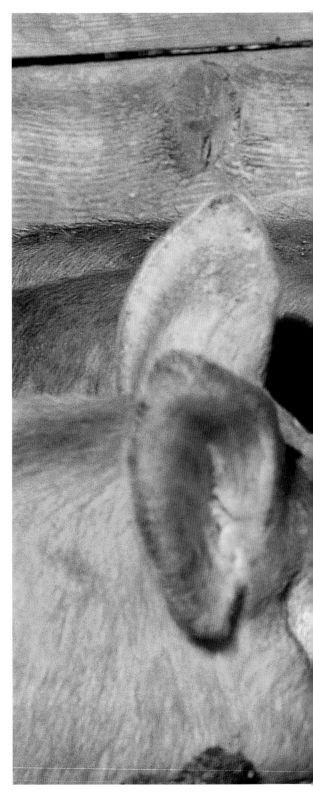

Chasing a greased pig came from the ancient English sport of pigrunning, which involved a large greased pig with its tail cut short. The pig was let loose and became the possession of whichever agile man or boy could catch the pig and hold it by the tail above his head.

Another sport involving pigs and grease is also of English origin: A small pig was inserted in a box with a door in the bottom, and the door was fastened with a catch. This box was placed at the edge of a large water tank. A greased pole was placed across the tank from the box to the other side. Make it across the greased pole, release the pig from the box, and the pig was yours. All too often both contestant and pig ended up taking a swim.

Chasing greased pigs

Greased pig races still exist in the United States where they are highlights at state and county fairs. This tradition began when an eighty pound pig coated with axle grease or crude oil was startled by the shot of a pistol at least twenty-five yards in front of a mob of eager pursuers. Races would last for as long as twenty to thirty minutes before the greased pig—not so greasy after having been grabbed at and hugged by enough clutching hands—was sufficiently exhausted that it could be caught. (Photograph © Keith Baum/BaumsAway!)

137

Tired trio
The sun is warm, but the mud is cool—a tired trio finds the ideal place for an afternoon nap. (Photograph © Alan and Sandy Carey)

Pig-mania: Collecting Pig Paraphernalia

Collectors of pig miscellany thrill to anything remotely resembling swine, with pig cookie jars and piggy banks among the most popular collectibles. Figurines of kissing pigs, chubby piglets, pigs dressed as cooks, wind-up pigs, antique pig mementoes, or pig T-shirts are always in hot demand.

The "Happy Pig Collectors" is a group of cheerful folks who love pigs and love to have anything pig-related in their possession. They enjoy getting together at a convention once a year to share unusual and antique pig collectibles. The organization, based in Oneida, Illinois, has a current membership of around 150 swineophiles who live in thirty-two states, plus Canada and Australia. The group has a quarterly newsletter called *The Happy Pig*, through which members share information on unusual pig items and network with others who share their obsession.

Betsy Williamson and her parents are typical Happy Pig Collectors. "We've never counted, but I would estimate that there are at least 2,000 pigs in our collection, probably more," she says. "The most unique one is the real pig that we had freeze-dried—just like those coyotes and squirrels that you see in museum displays, lots of times they have been freeze-dried—by a local business. The pig now resides in a custom-built case in my parents' basement."

(Happy Pig Collectors Club logo used with permission. Pig collectibles from the collection of Gene Holt)

Are you my mother?
Sometimes swine management requires a steady
hand and tender touch. (Photograph © J. C.
Allen & Son, West Lafayette, IN)

139

Reading and References

Baring-Gould, Rev. S. *The Lives of the Saints*. Edinburgh, Scotland: J. Grant, 1914.

Bertram, Anne. *Aw Shucks: The Dictionary of Country Jawing*. Lincolnwood, Ill.: NTC Publishing Group, 1997.

Bettleheim, Bruno. *The Uses of Enchantment: The Meaning and Importance of Fairy Tales*. New York: Vintage Books, 1977.

Bewick, Thomas. *A General History of Quadrupeds*. Newcastle upon Tyne, England: S. Hodgson, R. Beilby, and T. Bewick, 1790.

Bonera, Franco. *Pigs: Art, Legend, History*. Boston: Bullfinch Press, 1991.

Bowman, Sarah. *Pigs*. New York: Macmillan, 1981.

Brewer, Rev. Ebenezer Cobham. *A Dictionary of Phrase and Fable*. Centenary ed. London: Cassell, 1971.

Briggs, Hilton M. *International Pig Breed Encyclopedia*. Indianapolis, Ind.: Elanco Animal Health, 1983.

Briggs, Katherine M. *A Dictionary of British Folktales*. Bloomington: Indiana University Press, 1970.

Cassidy, Frederick G. et al., eds. *Dictionary of American Regional English*, Vols. 1, 2, and 3. Cambridge, Mass.: Belknap Press of Harvard, 1986, 1991, 1996.

Cavendish, Richard, ed. *Man, Myth, & Magic: An Illustrated Encyclopedia of the Supernatural*. New York: Marshall Cavendish, 1970.

CNN. *Earth Matters* (television documentary), broadcast July 9, 1998.

Coburn, F. D. *Swine in America*. New York: Orange Judd Co., 1909.

Conway, D. J. *Animal Magick: The Art of Recognizing and Working With Familiars*. St. Paul, Minn.: Llewellyn Publications, 1995.

Ensminger, M. E. and R. O. Parker. *Swine Science*. 5th ed. Danville, Ill.: The Interstate Printers and Publishers, 1984.

Evans, E. P. *Animal Symbolism in Ecclesiastical Architecture*. London: Heineman, 1896.

Fricke, Mary Elizabeth. *Dino, Godzilla, and the Pigs: My Life on Our Missouri Hog Farm*. New York: Soho Press, 1993.

Gaffney, Sean and Seamus Cashman, eds. *Proverbs and Sayings of Ireland*. County Dublin, Ireland: The Wolfhound Press, 1974.

Goodale, Jane C. *To Sing With Pigs Is Human: The Concept of Person in Papua New Guinea*. Seattle: University of Washington Press, 1995.

Hall, S. J. G. and J. Clutton-Brock. *Two Hundred Years of British Farm Livestock*. London: British Museum, 1989.

Halliwell, J. O. *Nursery Rhymes and Nursery Tales*. London: n.p., 1843.

Harris, Joseph. *Harris on the Pig*. New York: Orange Judd Co., 1870.

Harris, Marvin. *Cows, Pigs, Warriors, and Witches: The Riddles of Culture*. New York: Random House, 1974.

Hedgepeth, William. *The Hog Book*. Athens: University of Georgia Press, 1998.

Henderson, Andrew. *Scottish Proverbs*. Glasgow, Scotland: Thomas D. Morison, 1881.

Jacobs, Joseph. *English Fairy Tales*. London: David Nutt, 1895.

Jay, Ricky. *Learned Pigs and Fireproof Women*. New York: Villard Books, 1987.

Klingender, Francis. *Animals in Art and Through to the End of the Middle Ages*. Cambridge, Mass.: MIT Press, 1971.

Klober, Kelly. *A Guide to Raising Pigs: Care, Facilities, Breed Selection, Management (Storey Animal Handbook)*. Pownal, Vt.: Storey Books, 1998.

Leach, Maria, ed. *Funk & Wagnalls Standard Dictionary of Folklore, Mythology and Legend*. New York: Funk & Wagnalls, 1940–1950.

Levine, Philip. *Not This Pig*. Middletown, Conn.: Wesleyan University Press, 1966.

Long, James. *The Book of the Pig*. London: Upcott Gill, 1902.

Malcolmson, Robert and Stephanos Mastoris. *The English Pig: A History*. London: Hambledon Press, 1998.

Mason, Ian L. *World Dictionary of Livestock Breeds*. 3rd ed. Oxfordshire, England: C.A.B. International, 1983.

Nissenson, Marilyn and Susan Jonas. *The Ubiquitous Pig*. New York: Harry N. Abrams, 1996.

Pig Parade. London: Elm Tree Books, 1985.

Pond, W. G. *The Biology of the Pig*. Ithaca, N.Y.: Cornell University Press, 1978.

Porter, Valerie. *Pigs: A Handbook to the Breeds of the World*. Ithaca, N.Y.: Cornell University Press, 1993.

Potter, Beatrix. *The Tale of Pigling Bland*. 1913. Reprint, New York and London: Frederick Warne & Co., 1987.

Rawson, Jessica, ed. *Animals in Art*. London: British Museum, 1977.

Ray, J. Reverend. *A Compleat Collection of English Proverbs*. n.p.: J. Hughes, 1737.

Scott, Jack Denton. *The Book of the Pig*. New York: G. P. Putman, 1981.

Sidney, Samuel. *The Pig*. London: Routledge, Warne & Routledge. 1871.

Sillar, F. C. and R. M. Meyler. *The Symbolic Pig*. Edinburgh and London: Oliver & Boyd Ltd., 1961.

Stevenson, Burton, ed. *The Macmillan Book of Proverbs, Maxims & Famous Phrases*. New York: Macmillan, 1966.

Tallman, Marjorie. *Dictionary of American Folklore*. New York: Philosophical Library, 1959.

Towne, Charles W. and Edward N. Wentworth. *Pigs From Cave to Cornbelt*. Norman: University of Oklahoma Press, 1950.

Vince, John Norman Thatcher. *Old British Livestock: Shire Album 5*. [London]: Shire Publications, Ltd., 1976.

Winfrey, Laurie Platt. *Pig Appeal*. New York: Walker and Company, 1982.

Wiscombe, Martin. *The Old Pig*. Oxford, England: Past Times, 1996.

Wiseman, Julian. *A History of the British Pig*. [London]: Duckworth, 1988.

Youatt, William. *The Pig*. New York: n.p., 1847.

Index

About the Author

Author Sara Rath with original pig sculpture by Henri Studio, Wauconda, Illinois. (Photograph by Nancy Rubly)

Sara Rath admits that her personal relationship with pigs has been rather limited, but she feels comfortable researching and writing about them. Born and raised in Manawa, Wisconsin, a small town in the central part of the state, the rural landscape of her youth has influenced much of her personal life and creative work. Previous books on cows (*About Cows*, 1987, and *The Complete Cow*, 1998) proved extremely popular with readers and reviewers. Sara has freelanced and authored prizewinning books and projects in a variety of genres, including television drama and documentaries. She was awarded a Wisconsin Arts Board Fellowship for her fiction, and fellowships for residencies at The MacDowell Colony and The Ucross Foundation for her poetry. Sara is married to Del Lamont. They reside in Elm Grove, a suburb of Milwaukee, where their home welcomes visits by their combined family of six children and thirteen grandchildren.

The Tail End
A couple of "buttinskis" pigging out. (Photograph © Jim Steinbacher, courtesy of Leslie Levy Creative Art Licensing, Scottsdale, AZ)